MW01045768

How to Eat Out in Portugal & Brazil

*How to understand the menu
and make yourself understood*

Dictionary and Phrase Book
for the Restaurant

GREMESE

Originally published as:
Portogallo e Brasile al Ristorante

© 1996 L'Airone Editrice
P.O.Box 14237
00149 Rome – Italy

English translation:
Elizabeth Harrowell

Jacket design:
Carlo Soldatini

Photocomposition:
Graphic Art 6 s.r.l. – Rome

Printed and bound by:
SO.GRA.TE. – Città di Castello (PG)

© 1997 Gremese International s.r.l.
P.O. Box 14335
00149 Rome - Italy

ISBN 88-7301-100-4

Portugal and Brazil are closely linked by their common history of colonization and by many historical events influencing their economic and social development.

For this reason, as well as for the language they have in common, we have put them together in this book although they are widely different from the point of view of the food, or rather of their eating habits, as you will see in the following pages.

In Portugal fishing and the cultivation of olives and vines were already well developed by the eighth century and today are among the most important economic activities. To this nation of sailors goes the merit of having introduced into Europe a variety of spices and products such as coffee, tea, chili, curry, rice, and many more. *Tradition* and *care*: these are the two words which define Portuguese food.

It is a tradition which has managed to hold its own against the invasion of frozen foods and fast food establishments thanks to its rich variety. Each region, and even each single family, is able to add to any single recipe that touch of individuality which goes to make a genuinely "typical" dish. Just think – one of the "Kings" of French gastronomy produced a summary of his country's regional cookery in 325 recipes, while the most complete Portuguese cookery books include at least 800 specialties. It is a tradition well appreciated by those who enjoy good food.

Page after page could be devoted to typically Brazilian food which has been enriched with new ideas and ingredients contributed by the peoples and ethnic groups present within its borders. Portuguese, African, Indian and European influences in its architecture, its life-style, and in the faces of its people, are also reflected in the realm of food. A single gastronomic identity is unlikely to be found in such an enormous country; and the climate, so decisive in forming eating habits, varies in Brazil from temperate to tropical, from drought to freezing temperatures in the South. Generally speaking, the North and North East offer the best in the way of fish and seafood, while in the South meat is the main food. The big cities are in central-southern Brazil, and there the routine and stress of everyday life have almost succeeded in eclipsing the delights of the table. In spite of this, these areas have kept alive the local traditions with familiar, substantial, genuine dishes such as the famous *feijoada*.

This guide offers its readers the opportunity to appreciate the best of Portuguese and Brazilian food by introducing them to the main features, the most typical dishes and ingredients; it also provides some of the original recipes which can be easily prepared at home after the journey.

(Portuguese dishes are indicated with a **P**, Brazilian ones with a **B**.)

MAIN CHARACTERISTICS

Clearly the specialties presented in this book represent only the main features of the regional cookery; the real quality of the foods eaten will depend not only on the area visited but also, and mainly, on the restaurant selected.

The basic ingredients of Portuguese cookery – the fish, the meat, the vegetables – are in the main local produce.

Throughout the country, one of the typical features is the almost daily habit of eating soup, rice or potatoes (cooked in the usual ways) and sweets (mostly made from eggs).

In spite of its relatively small size, Portugal's several regions all boast their own separate gastronomic identity; salted cod, however, is to be found everywhere; it is the national dish and, according to popular tradition, can be cooked in 365 different ways, one for every day of the year.

Portuguese cookery includes both marvelous dishes of fish

and seafood, and fillings of pork and lamb or of local game. As in the Mediterranean countries, cheeses, sausages and ham, bread and wines are all essential components of the diet, and typical local products of excellent quality are to be found in all regions. Mealtimes are a source of great pleasure to the Portuguese. Brazilian cookery varies widely from place to place, and your opinion on local food will also depend to a great extent on your personal curiosity in the matter of experimenting with new flavors; in the kitchen, tradition gives way to the creativity favored by tropical tastes.

However large the menu in your chosen restaurant may be, it can in no way offer a collection of all the country's gastronomic features. The northern part of the country, which includes the Amazon area, offers many exotic foods, from small turtles to crabs, while in the north-eastern part (now the part most frequently "explored" by tourists) the choice is bewilderingly wide amongst the wonderful fish and seafood delicacies so strongly influenced by Afro-Indian features. The central-western regions consisting of such extreme contrasts as the country's capital, Brasilia, and the Pantanal of Mato Grosso, offer numerous dishes based on local game, including venison and paca meat. At the other end of the country, the south-eastern region offers a fairly international cuisine with meat as its most important feature; the predominance of meat dishes is found in the South as well, with many variations particularly among the vegetable dishes.

Fruit, juices and salads are available no matter the season, from north to south; beer, always chilled, and *cafezinho* are drunk several times a day.

The menu

Both in Portugal and in Brazil, a typical meal is made up of three or four dishes plus dessert.

In both countries you start with a *couvert* (an aperitif) which will normally include olives, paté, butter or cheese, bread or croutons, ham and pickles. Restaurants often put bread on the table without it being ordered, especially in Portugal where it is an integral part of the meal and where a wide variety is available. After that, there may be a starter, for example seafood or soup or many other options offered by the restaurant. Then the choice is between fish and meat, or even both (in which case the fish precedes the meat). In some places you can ask for half portions in order to taste several different specialties.

Each dish of fish or meat is served with rice, potatoes or pasta, and sometimes with vegetables or salad as well. It is therefore advisable to ask for full details before ordering too much. In any case, the waiter will probably suggest salad at the beginning of the meal. In the most traditional Portuguese restaurants there will be local cheeses to try at the end of the meal as well.

At this point you still have a dessert, fresh fruit, or ice cream to choose from. And at last you are free to conclude with coffee and a liqueur. In Brazil, the coffee is generally offered with the compliments of the restaurant.

Restaurants in Portugal

The variety of restaurants in Portugal offers something to suit all tastes and all pocketbooks.

Nearly all hotels also have a restaurant, generally with good service; however if one's aim is to try the best of local dishes, it is advisable to give some thought to the choice of where to eat. In the cities there are top-class places with top-class prices, specializing in both national and international cuisine and offering an enormous selection of wines. In Lisbon, near the Bairro Alto, there are places where you can enjoy a performance of *fado* while having an excellent dinner.

Eating places in a different category are to be found more or less everywhere, the simpler taverns (*tabernas*) with more genuine food and fairly good prices (depending of course on currency exchange rates). It goes without saying that the atmosphere in these places is not particularly elegant, but the simplicity and friendliness of those present will put you at your ease.

We advise you to avoid places offering a tourist menu, frequently poor in the quality/price ratio; on the other hand, it is advisable to pay attention to the day's specialty that they recommend. Prices are reasonable on the whole, although they vary according to the type of restaurant and the area (cheaper inland, in the North and on the central coast). Normally a complete meal, wine included, will cost between 2,000 and 2,500 escudos (approximately US$ 13-16.00). It is not normally necessary to book a table, but restaurants in the most popular tourist resorts may be crowded especially on weekends, so in this case it is best to phone or drop in to make a reservation.

In the cities, most restaurants accept international credit cards but you should take cash when going to smaller places. Service is included in the bill, but most customers leave a tip of 5-10% of the amount.

RESTAURANTS IN BRAZIL

It is hardly necessary to say that there is a wide variety of restaurants in Brazil. To enable you to choose more easily, you can find restaurant guides sold at newsstands or else get a weekly paper containing information on quality, prices, menus and addresses of the restaurants in town.

It is more than likely that your hotel will offer at least a breakfast service. It is usually quite a substantial meal with different types of fruit and tropical juices, jams, brioches, coffee, etc.

During the day, on the beaches of the towns and holiday resorts there are kiosks (*barraquinhas*) ready to serve tasty snacks and tropical drinks. You should agree on the price before ordering. In the North East, get somebody local to advise you on a restaurant with good prices and quality. If you are in Rio or São Paulo you will have no difficulty in finding restaurants with international food. The same cities also have a number of restaurants of a particular type, such as a fixed-price buffet or with prices by weight, and the *rodizio di massas* (different types of pasta served one after the other). The chains of *churrascarias*, temples to roast meat, are to be found in all the main cities, and they often put on samba shows or live music for their patrons.

Until a few years ago, travelling in Brazil was an even more economical experience as seafood was available at ridiculously low prices. This changed somewhat in mid-1994 when the economy was "dollarized" and prices went up. Today the average price of a complete meal, drinks and service included, is about R$ 25, (about US$ 27). This will obviously be affected by various factors such as the region and the kind of menu and the restaurant you choose. Since the bill nearly always includes a 10% service charge, you are not obliged to tip, though it is customary. Credit cards are widely accepted.

On Friday and Saturday evenings, at midday on Sundays and on public holidays, restaurants are generally crowded, so it is a good idea to book, perhaps through your hotel.

Now, to get your mouth really watering, read on... *Bom apetite!*

Cheeses in Portugal are highly valued, and quite a good variety is available. Unlike some countries, cheese is used not so much as an ingredient but as a food in its own right, at the beginning or at the end of a meal (particularly in cold weather and in country areas).

Portuguese cheeses are of different types: made from cow's milk, sheep's milk, fresh, seasoned, flakey, fat, spicy... The best known are those produced traditionally in the central-southern inland areas of the country, but it is always a good idea to ask for cheese produced locally, wherever you may be.

In Brazil, cheese is much less fat and more frequently produced industrially for climatic and cultural reasons. It is more commonly used in snacks and on pasta dishes in those areas around São Paulo where there is a large Italian population. The State of Minas Gerais, between Rio de Janeiro and São Paulo, has the best-developed production of cheese in the nation, including European kinds such as camembert, gouda, provolone, gruyère and so on. In both Portugal and Brazil, however, traditionally Italian and French cheeses are produced: provolone, gorgonzola, mozzarella (*mussarela*) parmesan, brie and Roquefort.

This is a list of the most typical cheeses, each with a short description:

Alandroal *ahlahndroo<u>a</u>l* (**P**): This is produced in the area south of Lisbon, Alentejo. It is a compact goat's milk cheese, the color varying from white to pale yellow according to the length of seasoning it has undergone. The flavor and smell are strong.

Azeitão *ahzeh-eet<u>a</u>oon* (**P**): Small, creamy goat's milk cheeses with a particular flavor. They are preferably eaten during the spring. They come from various areas including Azeitão in the coastal area near Lisbon.

CHEESES

Catupiry *kahtoopee<u>ree</u>* (**B**): Produced in the Minas Gerais area, it is a fresh fat cheese made from cow's milk, pale in color and soft. It is an ingredient in a number of dishes and is also used on pizza.

Queijo da Ilha <u>keh</u>-eejoo dah <u>ee</u>lya (**P**): This highly flavored cheese is produced on the island of Pico, one of the nine islands of the Azores. It is a hard cheese and is grated for use in regional cookery. On the island it is eaten with the local maize bread.

Queijo da Serra <u>keh</u>-eejoo dah <u>se</u>hra (**P**): This is the best-known Portuguese cheese. It is still produced by local people in the Serra da Estrela, Portugal's highest mountain range. Made from sheep's milk, yellowish and soft in texture with a delicate flavor, it is somewhat similar to the best brie. It is mostly eaten in winter and gains its full flavor when accompanied by Port wine.

Queijo Minas <u>keh</u>-eejoo <u>mee</u>nash (**B**): As its name shows, it is from the Minas Gerais region. It is made from cow's milk and is pure white, fat free and delicately flavored, slightly salted and either creamy or more compact in texture. It is eaten at breakfast or lunch and is good for those on a diet.

Queijo Prato <u>keh</u>-eejoo <u>pra</u>htoo (**B**): Produced throughout the country it is in fact a more industrialized version of gouda. In color yellow, it is nearly always sold in slices as it used in the making of lasagne and sandwiches.

Requeijão *rehkeh-eej<u>a</u>oon* (**B**): A very common cheese from cow's milk, white, very creamy and quite rich with a sweet flavor. It is used a good deal in sauces and in other dishes, but it is also eaten at breakfast on bread with jam.

Ricota *reekohtah* (**B**): Similar to the Italian ricotta cheese, it is made from cow or goat's milk, creamy and delicate, and must be eaten while it is still fresh. It is used in baking, both sweet and savory, and in small cakes.

Serpa *serpah* (**P**): A cheese from Alentejo. Sweet in flavor, it is oily when fresh but becomes dry and strongly flavored after a year or two of seasoning.

In Portugal even the best cuts of pork and other meats are made into tasty dried meats using traditional methods. In some places such as the Alentejo in central-southern Portugal, dried sausage and bread are the basic foods of the local population.

Brazil, on the other hand, is not traditionally a great consumer of these products. Those produced industrially, like cooked ham and dried sausage are mainly used in sandwiches and in the preparation of a few dishes. *Linguiça* (*lingweessah*), small, soft sausages are common while hams and sausages are found in Italian and German restaurants as well as in the Portuguese ones, and in the southern part of the country.

The following is a small selection of Portuguese cold cut meats, as those made in Brazil do not possess specifically individual features.

Alheiras *ahlyeh-eerash*: These tasty sausages from the North contain chicken, rabbit and pork together with bread, garlic, pepper, and olive oil. They are eaten fried, often as a complete meal with potatoes and vegetables.

Bexiga *besheegah*: This highly flavored sausage is made from the bladder and loin of the pig with onion and blood. It is produced and eaten mainly in the North East.

Cacholeira *kashooleh-eerah*: This sausage made from pig's liver and garlic wrapped in thin tripe is made in the Alentejo area. Its fragrance and flavor are distinctive.

Chouriça de sangue *showreessoo deh sangeh*: These dried sausages are made from fatty pork and cooked blood which give them a dark color and strong flavor.

Chouriços *showreessoosh*: Produced almost all over the country, these are made from pig's flesh, nerves and blood with garlic, peppers and white wine added, wrapped in cow's tripe.

Farinheiras *fareenyeh-eerash*: Sausages made from the belly and breast of the pig, dressed with garlic, saffron and flour. From central Portugal, they are fried, or used as a complete meal with rice or potatoes.

Linguiças *lingweessash*: Small sausages produced in the North and in the Alentejo region from nerveless pork, a little red wine, garlic, and salt.

Paios *pah-yoosh*: Dried sausages made from lean pork, easily digestible, flavored with garlic and salt and contained in pig's skin.

Presunto *prezoontoo*: Raw ham mainly from the North East and Center South, made in the traditional way and eaten the year after production. By the way, *presunto* means cooked ham in Brazil, which is *fiambre* in Portugal.

SWEETS AND PASTRIES

As mentioned, in Portugal sweets almost always containing egg are favorites. On the other hand, in Brazil the preference goes to fresh sweets such as mousse and fruit flans, as well as ice-creams and jellies. Both countries therefore offer an interesting and wide variety of desserts. Here is our choice:

Aletria *ahlehtreeah* (**P**): This is a typical Portuguese sweet from the North. Thin strips of pasta are cooked in milk with egg yolk and sugar, served sprinkled with cinnamon.

Arroz-doce *arosh dosseh* (**P**): From the North to the South, the country boasts at least eight variations of this rice pudding cooked in the same way as the *aletria*, and even more popular.

Baba-de-moça *bahbah djee mossah* (**B**): A cream from Bahia made from coconut milk, egg yolk and sugar. It can be eaten alone (see "Recipes") or used in the preparation of other sweets.

Bolinhos *booleenyoosh* (**P**): This is the name for small cakes. An ample variety are found in the cakeshops *(pastelarias)* all over the country, some filled with cream, some with dried fruit.

Bolinhos de Jerimu *booleenyoosh deh jereemoo* (**P**): Fried sweets made from pumpkin, egg and Port wine.

Bolo Rei *bohloo rey* (**P**): It is made from spongelike dough baked in the oven containing dried fruit, egg, orange and lemon juice, and Port wine. It is eaten at Christmas all over the country, although it came from the Lisbon area originally.

Brigadeiro *brigahdeyroo* (**B**): Small sweets much loved by children made from condensed milk and chocolate, and covered with grated chocolate. *Cajuzinhos* are very similar, but contain chestnuts as well.

Cajuzinhos *cajoozeenyoss* (**B**): See *Brigadeiro* above.

Canjica *kanjeekah* (**B**): A sweet from Bahia made from green cobs of maize with sugar and cinnamon.

Cocada *kokahdah* (**B**): This sweet made with grated coconut is from Bahia. Its consistency and color (which can be light or dark) vary according to how long the sugar is cooked.

Dolce de ovos *dohsseh deh ohvoosh* (**P**): Small sweets of egg yolk and sugar which in their original form are from the town of Aveiro. They are served as a dessert, or used as a filling for cakes, or wrapped in wafers in various shapes.

Geléias *djehlehyas* (**B**): Jams which can be made from a variety of fruits. All flavors are available: papaya, pineapple, banana, *goiaba*, *jaca*, *caju* and so on.

Manjar *manjar* (**B**): A type of pudding made of coconut and coconut milk; it is normally served with a plum dessert.

Pão-de-ló *paoon deh loh* (**P**): Similar to a sponge cake and homemade rather than factory produced. It is rich in egg yolk, butter and sugar.

Pastel de Belém *pashtel deh behlehm* (**P**): See *Pastel de natas* below.

Pastel de natas *pashtel deh nahtash* (**P**): Small pastries filled with cinnamon-flavored cream. They are also known as *pastel de Belém* because they come from the Belém district in Lisbon.

Pastel de Santa Clara *pasht<u>e</u>l deh s<u>a</u>hntah kl<u>a</u>hra* (**P**): Puff pastries from North East Portugal, star shaped and filled with a cream made of egg yolks and almonds.

Pavê *pav<u>e</u>h* (**B**): Fruit or chocolate are added to a custard cream with sweet biscuits in this dessert (see "Recipes").

Quindim *kindj<u>ee</u>n* (**B**): A superb sweet with grated coconut, egg yolk and sugar; it is creamy on top and crispier towards the bottom. It can come in individual portions or else as a full-size sweet (*Quindão*).

Rabanadas *rahbahn<u>a</u>hdash* (**P**): Made of slices of bread soaked in milk or wine, coated in sugar then fried. They are eaten sprinkled with sugar and cinnamon, generally in winter.

Rocambole *rokanb<u>oh</u>lee* (**B**): This sweet is a pastry roll filled with *goiabadah* (jam made of local fruit).

Tapioca *tapy<u>o</u>kah*: In Portugal, tapioca is cooked in practically the same way as *aletria*, whereas in Brazil this sweet is made with uncooked tapioca covered with condensed milk, coconut milk, grated coconut and sugar.

Tortas *t<u>o</u>rtash* (**B**): In Brazil cakes and sweets are more popular than small cakes and pastries. They are cooked in many different ways, the most popular being chocolate, lemon, coconut and cheesecakes.

Toucinho do céu *toh-ooss<u>ee</u>nyoo doo s<u>eh</u>-oo*: This sweet is made from egg yolks and almonds, filled with a cream of green pumpkin. According to tradition the original version came from Alentejo in southern Portugal, though there are other versions in the North and in the central regions of the country.

Portugal is well known for the quality of its wines (*vinhos*). From north to south, the country is rich in vineyards typical of the beautiful scenery everywhere. Apart from the famous Port and Madeira, there are more than a hundred different varieties of wine, both table wines and more special vintages which are the foremost export product of the nation.

Wines are classified as *verdes* or *maduros* (*branco* or *tinto*), *rosados* and *licorosos*: green wines or mature wines (whites or reds), rosé and liqueur wines. The so-called "green wine" is a wine of controlled origin (DOC) made from grapes that for climatic reasons have not fully ripened. It is only produced on the Costa Verde, the coastal region in the north of the country.

Like other tropical countries, Brazil does not have a great wine tradition except for the South, particularly in the region of the Rio Grande do Sul, where the climate is cool enough nearly all year round; here live many European families, Germans especially, who make various kinds of wine. Most of the foreign wine in Brazil comes from Portugal and Chile. The most popular drink of all is the national beer. (*Antartica, Kaiser,* and *Skol* are among the best-known brands.)

The following is a selection of the most popular Portuguese and Brazilian wines and liqueurs:

Amarguinha *ahmargeenyah* (**P**): A liqueur produced in the extreme south of Portugal, the Algarve. Made from bitter almonds, it is opaque, brown in color and has a bitter flavor. It is used as a digestive after meals.

Bagaço *bahgahssoo* (**P**): This drink is obtained by distilling fermented vegetable substances; like aquavitae (*aguardente*), it can reach 70 degrees alcohol content.

Bairrada *baeerahdah* (**P**): A vintage wine, either white or red, produced on the Costa da Prata (the Silver Coast). It is of a quality suited to accompany regional dishes such as fish soup (see *Caldeirada* in "National Dishes"), fresh sardines, or roast Coimbra pork.

Batida *bahteedah* (**P**): See *Cachaça* below.

Bucelas *boosselash* (**P**): A white wine from the town of the same name near Lisbon. It is slightly acid when new but becomes dry in aging. It is served chilled and generally accompanies roast fish.

Cachaça *kashahssah* (**B**): This aquavitae from sugar cane can be drunk straight but is mainly used in the preparation of typical drinks such a *caipirinha* with sugar, lemon and ice, and *batida* with tropical fruit juice or coconut milk.

Casa da Calçada, Casal Garcia, Casal Mendes *kahza dah kalssahdah, kahzal garsseeah, kahzal mehndesh* (**P**): "Green wines," with low alcohol content and slightly sparkling. The whites go well with seafood and white fish, while the reds are served with starters of liver paté, olives and so on.

Château Duvalier (**B**): It is one of the best and most famous wines produced in the South of Brazil. It comes in the three versions, white, rosé and red, and is drunk on special occasions such as weddings, birthdays and the like.

Caipirinha *kaeepireenyah* (**B**): See *Cachaça* above.

Colares *koolahresh* (**P**): Mature, light wines from the coastal area north of Lisbon. The red is served at room temperature with red meat; the white, always well cooled, is best with fish, pasta and strongly flavored cheeses.

Conhaque _kon<u>yak</u>_: Made from the distillation of matured wines which thus become brandy with an alcohol content of between 38 and 45 degrees. The most famous brands are _A Macieira_ (_ah mass<u>yeh</u>-eerah_) in Portugal and _Dreher_ in Brazil.

Dão _d<u>aoon</u>_ (**P**): These are mature wines from the central-eastern part of the country, the Beira Alta. The flavor is mellow, with an alcohol content of 11-13 degrees. The reds are served with spicy meat dishes while the more delicate and aromatic whites are good with roast meats and strong cheeses.

Gatão _ght<u>aoon</u>_ (**P**): A "green wine" (see above), with a lightly citrus flavor, well known and appreciated mainly in the white version.

Ginginha _jeenj<u>een</u>yah_ (**P**): A strong liqueur made from cherries and produced in the small town of Alcobaça on the central coast. It is served after the meal.

Lagos _lah<u>goosh</u>_ (**P**): Wines from the Algarve in the far south of Portugal. Full bodied and clear, their alcohol content is over 13 degrees. The reds go well with roast meats and salted cod, while the whites are used as an aperitif or together with the starters.

Madeira _mah<u>deh</u>-eerah_ (**P**): Together with Port, this wine has made the name of Portuguese wines. It has been produced on Madeira more or less from the time that the island was first discovered more than four centuries ago. The alcohol content is quite high, from 14 to 18 degrees, and the wine is used as an aperitif or else after the meal, and it has endless uses in cookery (see "National Dishes"). Its main characteristic is the aging at a high temperature in special ovens. There are four types: *Boal*, semi-sweet and thick; *Verdelho*, semi-dry and dark; *Sercial*, dry and stronger; and *Malvasia*, the lightest and most aromatic.

Matheus Rosé *mahteh-oosh roseh* (**P**): This is probably the most popular of Portuguese rosé wines. It is a light wine with a pleasant flavor to accompany roast red meats and white meats cooked in every way.

Moscatel *mooshkahtehl* (**P**): This wine with a high alcohol content comes from the town of Setúbal, two hours from Lisbon. It is a sweet liqueur wine with a rich flavor, and is particularly esteemed when it reaches the age of twenty years. It is ideal served with, or after, dessert.

Porto *portoo* (**P**): The climate and particular techniques in the production have made this wine famous throughout the world for the last four centuries. It comes from the agricultural region of the Douro, near the town of Porto, and is produced with a rigorous process, strictly controlled at every step, which allows it to age for many years. There are two varieties, the white and the red, with the following characteristics:
– the white, while still young may be of a pale color, but it darkens slightly as it ages, becoming golden when it is at its best. It is served chilled as an aperitif;
– the red varies from a bright color when the wine is young and still sweet, to ruby (still sweet but after ten years' aging), to topaz (semi-dry, between the ages of ten and fifteen years therefore already considered top quality), right up to the clear golden red (the driest and the best, having reached the final stage of maturation in the barrel, a process which can take anything from twenty to forty years). It is sipped at room

temperature at the end of a meal, or else is accompanied by cheeses such as *Queijo da Serra* (see "Cheeses").

Sidra <u>see</u>drah (**B**): There are two types of cider, the natural one made from fermented apple juice which is slightly fizzy, then the *sidra champagne*, which is natural cider but with the addition of sugar and carbon dioxide. Cider is produced more in Brazil than in Portugal, and is drunk in particular on celebrations and holidays (birthdays, New Year, etc.) because it provides a cheaper alternative to the traditional champagne.

Verdelho *verde<u>h</u>lyoo* (**P**): This excellent wine is made on the island of Pico, one of the nine that make up the archipelago of the Azores. Dry and fairly dark, it accompanies regional dishes using pork and octopus.

OTHER SPECIALTIES

In this section we introduce some of the most intriguing examples of the Portuguese and Brazilian culinary art.

Bananas fritas *bahnahnash freetash* (**B**): This banana is of a variety known as "ground banana." It is sliced and fried in butter, and used to accompany a variety of dishes, or served alone sprinkled with sugar and cinnamon.

Bola de carne *bohla deh karneh* (**P**): This type of bread loaf is homemade, and is filled with meats (ham, veal, chicken, etc.), onion, tomato or other ingredients. It comes from the North and North East of the country.

Broa *broh-ah* (**P**): It is one of the most popular types of bread especially in northern and north-eastern Portugal. It is made from maize flour and is dark in color with a very hard crust; a sweet version also exists. The savory *broa* is eaten with different soups and main dishes, mainly the *Caldo verde* (see "National Dishes").

Caldo de cana *kahldoo djee kahnah* (**B**): This is a sweet, green juice extracted from sugar cane. It is prepared while you wait in roadside kiosks, and the custom is to drink it chilled as you eat a pancake with a *Minas* cheese filling (see "Cheeses").

Carne de sol or **Carne-seca** *karneh djee sohl* or *karneh sehkah* (**B**): Salted meat dried in the sun, very popular in the north-eastern regions and especially in the Bahia.

Palmito *pahlmeetoo* (**B**): These palm shoots look like short white sticks and have a very delicate, pleasant flavor; they are sold in jars or tins. They are eaten alone or in salads, or else are used in the preparation of risotto and sauces.

Pãozinho de queijo _paoonzeenyoo djee keh-eejoo_ (**B**): Small rolls containing grated cheese and baked in the oven. They are served hot as a snack or else as starters. They are extremely popular, so much so that some shops sell nothing but these.

Vinho quente _veenyoo kehnteh_ (**P**): Warmed wine, Madeira or Moscatel, sweet red Port (see "Wines and Spirits"), with egg yolk, sugar and tiny pieces of bread. It originated in the north of the country and according to tradition it accompanies fried sweets after midnight Mass at Christmas.

In this section we present some of the gastronomic terms that are most frequently found on the menu in Portuguese and Brazilian restaurants, so that you may order the food you wish understanding exactly what you are asking for.

À americana *ah ahmerikahnah*: With tomato and roast bacon and French fries. This will generally indicate the food accompanying a steak.

À andaluza *ah ahndahlooza*: A vegetable or a sauce made from stuffed eggplant or bell peppers.

À belle munière *ah behl moonyer*: A sauce based on button mushrooms, shrimps, and herbs browned in butter, a common dressing for fish dishes.

À caçadora *ah kahssahdorah*: A sauce made with wine, ham, tomato, parsley and mushrooms browned in butter, often to go with steaks and escalopes.

À Califórnia *ah kahleefornyah*: A sauce made from various fruits (apples, peaches, oranges and plums), with white wine and bacon, which nearly always accompanies the Christmas duck or turkey, sometimes as a stuffing.

À moda de ... *ah mohdah de ...* : This term is followed by a place name and indicates that the dish originated there.

À provençal *ah prohvehnssahl*: Garlic and egg yolk mixture.

Agridoce *ahgreehdosseh*: A sweet-and-sour dressing.

Ao champignon *shampeenyohn*: A sauce made from button mushrooms, butter and Madeira wine, normally accompanying veal slices or steaks.

GASTRONOMIC TERMS

Ao creme *ah-oo krehm*: The term means "with cream" and indicates a type of custard cream made with eggs, sugar and brandy.

Ao curry *ah-oo ker-ry*: With curry. This curry sauce is used especially with chicken dishes.

Ao thermidor *ah-oo termeedor*: This refers to lobster Thermidor cooked whole in the oven, with a sauce made from mustard, cream and grated cheese.

Assado *ahssahdoo*: This refers to meat roasted in the oven, frequently accompanied by roast potatoes. Roast meat and fish are very popular especially in Portugal.

Bife à cavalo *beefeh ah kahvahloo*: A steak with garlic, salt and pepper, cooked in butter with one or two fried eggs on it.

Caldo / Canja *kahldoo / kahnjah*: Both soups, but while the *caldo* is generally creamier, the *canja,* normally made from chicken, is more like a clear broth.

Cozido *koozeedoo*: This is an adjective which refers to any cooked ingredient.

Da casa / do chefe *dah kahzah / doo shehf*: This expression means that the dish is an invention of that particular restaurant or of that particular chef.

Flambado *flahnbahdoo*: The term corresponds to the French *flambé*, and indicates food which is doused with liqueur (rum or cognac) at the moment of serving, then set a flame.

GASTRONOMIC TERMS

Frito / Grelhado _freetoo / grelyahdoo_: The former indicates fried food, in particular fish and meat, while the latter indicates foods cooked on the grill or in a pan practically without any fat at all.

Guisado / Estufado _geesahdoo / stoofahdoo_: These expressions are limited almost completely to Portugal and refer to a method of braising the food, or some of the ingredients.

Juliana _joolyahna_: The expression nearly always refers to vegetables sliced into thin strips.

Manteiga _mahnteh-eegah_: A sauce with butter to accompany steak or roast fish.

Milanesa _meelahnehza_: Thin steaks or fish fillets floured, dipped in egg then in breadcrumbs and fried.

Molho Branco / Bechamel _mohlyoo brahnkoo / behshahmel_: White sauce prepared by hand from butter, Maizena flour, salt and nutmeg.

Mostarda _moostardah_: A sauce to go with steak and chips, made with hot mustard.

Na brasa _nah brahzah_: It refers to food cooked on the grill.

Noisette _nwazeht_: This is the name given to potatoes the size of nuts, small and round, browned in butter. They often accompany rabbit _à caçador_.

Parmegiana _parmehdjahnah_: This describes a fried steak covered with tomato sauce and melted cheese.

Piemontesa *pyehmohntehsah*: A creamy sauce made from butter, grated cheese, white truffle or button mushrooms, with a touch of liqueur wine. Rice à *piemontesa* is quite commonly served with steak in Brazil.

Provençal *proovehnssahl*: A sauce made from garlic, egg yolk, tomato and parsley.

Rosé *rohseh*: A cold sauce made from tomato purée (or ketchup) and cream. It is used especially in Brazil for salad and on croutons.

Steak au poivre: Steak with a sauce made with black peppercorns, accompanied by potatoes cooked then browned in the oven with Roquefort cheese.

Tártaro *tartahroo*: A cold dressing based on mayonnaise, spring onions, hard-boiled egg yolks and gherkins.

Vinagrete *veenagrehte*: A cold dressing for salad or roast fish, made with vinegar, olive oil, herbs and chopped onion.

NATIONAL DISHES

This section gives a small selection of the dishes or their ingredients found more or less everywhere in Brazil and Portugal. Each one, of course, comes from some specific area and no doubt there, special care is given to the dish and to the choice of ingredients. Nevertheless, there are some specialties so well known and popular that they are found in all parts of the country and can be considered fundamental in the gastronomic repertoire of both nations. This is especially true in Portugal; Brazil being so large, and the number of traditional influences as regards food so varied, that regional differences are more marked.

You will obtain further information on this subject from the sections on "Regional Dishes" and "Recipes."

PORTUGAL

Açorda *assorda*: A kind of toasted bread fried in olive oil and garlic, eaten alone or with one or more types of fish or seafood.

Atum or **peixe-espada grelhado** *ahtoon* or *peh-eesheh spahdah grelyahdoo*: Fresh sliced tuna or swordfish, roasted and served with boiled potatoes in a sauce of butter and parsley.

Bacalhau *bahkalyah-oo*: Salted cod is the most traditional of Portuguese dishes and is cooked in a number of different ways according to the region. Oil, garlic, onion and potatoes are the most usual ingredients for its preparation; the most popular recipes are À Zé do Pipo, À Brás, À Gomes da Sá, fried or roast (see "Regional Dishes").

Bolinhos de bacalhau *booleenyoosh deh bahkalyah-oo*: Fried croquettes of salted cod, potatoes, onions and parsley, often served at the beginning of the meal.

Caldeirada *kaldeh-eerahdah*: A kind of fish soup, generally rather spicy, made with various ingredients as well as a good variety of fish, or else only with sardines and salted cod. It may be a full meal or a starter according to the consistency and wealth of ingredients.

Caldo verde *kahldoo verdeh*: Soup prepared with a particular kind of locally grown cabbage called *couve galega*, sliced very finely and cooked with olive oil, onions, and potatoes. It is served with sliced dried sausage and a type of bread known as *broa* (see "Other Specialties").

Carne assada *karneh assahdah*: Goat, pork, veal or other kind of meat from a very young animal, roasted in the oven and served with roast or fried potatoes and vegetables.

Cozido à portuguesa *koozeedoo ah poortoogehzah*: Made with various meats (pork, beef, chicken and others), mixed with a good selection of vegetables cooked in the same water. The dish is accompanied by rice, and is served with bread and wine.

Melão com presunto *mehlaoon kohn prehzoontoo*: A refreshing starter; slices of melon wrapped in smoked ham.

Omelete *ohmehlehteh*: An omelette, either plain or else with a filling of cheese, ham, tomatoes, and other ingredients; even in the best restaurants it will be a full meal. It is served together with rice or fried potatoes and salad.

Rancho *rahnshoo*: White beans accompanied by carrots,

onion and pork, cooked with short pasta. Pieces of dried sausage and tripe are often added, especially in the region around the town of Porto.

Sardinhas *sard__ee__nyas*: Portuguese sardines are well known abroad where they are sold in olive oil in tins. In Portugal they are eaten fresh, roasted with tomato sauce, fried in batter, or preserved in oil or brine. They may be served as a starter or halfway through the meal, or else as a full meal in themselves accompanied by boiled potatoes in a butter and parsley sauce.

BRAZIL

Arroz com feijão *ar__o__sh kohn feh-eej__a__oon*: Rice with black beans browned in garlic, oil and onion. It is a simple but filling dish dating back to the age of slavery, and is still in daily use in Brazil accompanying meat and fish.

Camarão frito *kahmar__aoo__n fr__ee__too*: Fried whole prawns or shrimps. They are even served on the beaches accompanied by cool beer and dressed with chili oil, mayonnaise or other sauces.

Casquinhas de Siri *kashk__ee__nyash djee see__ree__*: Crab meat with several spices served in the shell. A starter.

Feijoada *feh-eejoo-__ahdah__*: The basic ingredient of this dish is black beans cooked with different meats and accompanied by rice, manioca flour and a kind of chicory browned in garlic and oil

Filé *feel__eh__*: Steaks, or veal or chicken slices fried and served with different kinds of sauces. It is accompanied by rice, beans, potatoes and salad.

Filé de peixe com molho de camarão *feeleh djee pe-eesheh kohn mohlyee-oo djee kahmaraoon*: Fillets or other cuts of fish (grouper or other kinds) with a shrimp sauce. The dish is served with rice.

Medalhão com arroz à piemontese *medahlyaoon con arosh ah pyemontehzeh*: A thick fillet steak wrapped in bacon and fried, accompanied by rice *à piemontese* (see "Gastronomic Terms").

Risoto *reezoh-toh*: Risotto prepared in a number of ways often accompanies meat and fish fillets.

Salada de macarrão *sahlahdah djee mahkaraoon*: A cold pasta salad eaten at the beginning of the meal; to the short pasta is added mayonnaise or cream, with raw vegetables (tomatoes, peas, carrots and so on) either grated or finely chopped.

Salada de palmito *salahda djee palmeetoo*: A salad made from palm shoots (see "Other Specialties"), an easily digestible, light ingredient, with an oil and vinegar dressing.

And now for a look at the main dishes listed according to their geographical origins, with a short description of the main ingredients and the method of preparation. However, bear in mind that endless variations are likely to exist.
At the beginning of the description you will find an indication as to whether the recipe is normally prepared as a starter or soup (S), as a main dish or complete meal (MD), or as an accompanying vegetable (V).
To make everything as clear as possible, we have divided the two nations geographically as follows:

Portugal:
The North (Minho and Douro)
The North East (Alto Douro and Trás-os-Montes)
The Center East (Beira Alta and Beira Baixa)
The Center West (Lisbon and hinterland: Estremadura and Ribatejo respectively)
The South (Alentejo)
The Far South (Algarve)
Madeira
The Azores

Brazil:
The North (the Amazon region, Manaus and Belém)
The North East (Recife, Fortaleza, Alagoas, Fernando de Noronha)
The Bahia Region
The Center West (Brasília, Mato Grosso and Goiás)
The Espírito Santo Region
The Minas Gerais Region
The Rio de Janeiro Region
The São Paulo Region
The South (Paraná, Santa Catarina, Rio Grande do Sul, Foz do Iguaçu)

REGIONAL DISHES

PORTUGAL

THE NORTH

This region is, historically, the one from which Portugal developed. The food is rich, as are the culinary traditions. More so than in the other regions, soup is eaten daily in the North, and there are many filling dishes both of meat and of fish. Magnificent local wines are always to be found at meals both in restaurants and in the home; special mention should be made of the "green wine" (see "Wines and Spirits"), and also of the regional sweets.

Some of the country's most popular dishes come from this area; among these we have chosen the following:

Arroz da pato *ar<u>o</u>sh deh <u>pa</u>htoo*: (MD) Risotto of strips of duck, containing preserved meats, onion, butter, and parsley.

Bacalhau à Gomes de Sá *bahkahly<u>aoo</u> ah <u>go</u>hmesh deh sah*: (MD) The flesh of salted cod in small pieces mixed with potatoes and cooked in olive oil, onions, eggs, milk and black olives.

Bacalhau à Margarida da Praça *bahkahly<u>aoo</u> ah margar<u>ee</u>dah dah <u>pra</u>hssah*: (MD) Pieces of salted cod, grilled and accompanied by potatoes and a sauce of olive oil and onions.

Bacalhau à Zé do Pipo *bahkahly<u>aoo</u> ah zeh doo <u>pee</u>poo*: (MD) Salted cod baked in the oven, with mashed potatoes and mayonnaise (see "Recipes").

Lampreia à moda do Minho *lamprehyah ah mohdah doo meenyoo*: (MD) The lamprey fish cooked in wine, olive oil, onion and various herbs, served with rice and toast.

Papas de sarrabulho *pahpash deh sarahboolyoo*: (S) A mixture of pig's liver, heart and other pork meats as well as fowl and beef, with pig's blood and cornflour added, to make a kind of thick soup to be eaten with toast.

Rancho *rahnshoo*: (MD) A dish consisting of a mixture of chickpeas, various meats (veal, beef, bacon) and short pasta.

Rojões *roojoeensh*: (MD) Mixed pork meats, marinated in wine, garlic and bay leaves, fried in its own fat and accompanied by roast chestnuts.

Roupa-velha *roh-oopah vehlyah*: (MD) Cooked salted cod leftovers, cabbage and potatoes, browned in garlic and olive oil.

Tripas à moda do Porto *treepash ah mohdah doo portoo*: (MD) Veal tripe with pork, cooked with lard, carrots, onions, and beans. It is accompanied by rice.

THE NORTH EAST

The North East is one of the poorest areas in Portugal. The basic food is game (partridge, rabbit, turkey and fowl) and local fish (trout), as well as pork and goat and their preserved meats. There are many wild mushrooms which often serve as an economical substitute to meat in the fall. In the southern part of the region along the River Douro, the economy is more advanced owing to the production of Port wine.

Bexiga *besheegah*: (MD) A variety of preserved pork sausage (see "Preserved Meats"), cooked and served with local greens called *grelos*.

Bola de presunto *bohlah deh prezoontoo*: (V) Homemade salted bread filled with fat ham, with extra-virgin olive oil.

Cabrito assado *kabreetoo assahdoo*: (MD) Roast kid goat stuffed with potatoes, olives and bacon. In this area, this dish never fails to appear at wedding feasts and on the table on Easter Sunday.

Carne de porco estufada com castanhas *karneh deh porkoo shtoofahdah kohn kashtahnyash*: Pig's trotter stewed with garlic, bay leaves and nutmeg, to which roast chestnuts are added at the last moment.

Cogumelos guisados *koogoomehloosh geesahdoosh:* (V) Two species of wild mushroom (called *pinheiros* and *cardielos*), browned in olive oil, onion, garlic and ham.

Feijoada à Transmontana *feh-eejooahdah ah transhmontahnah:* (MD) Different types of pork meat cooked with white beans, carrots and onions. The dish is served with rice.

Migas ripadas *meegash reepahdash*: (S) Slices of bread dampened with olive oil and flavored with browned garlic, accompanied by eggs fried in the same oil.

Perdiz com cogumelos *perdeesh kohn koogoomehloosh*: (MD) Partridge cut into pieces and cooked in olive oil with mushrooms and ham.

Peru assado no forno _pehroo assahdoo noo fornoo_: (MD)
Roast turkey stuffed with a sauce made from ham and eggs,
accompanied by a risotto made with the offal of the bird itself.

Sopa de alheiras _sohpah deh alyeh-eerash_: (S) Soup made
from _alheiras_ (a local dried sausage, see "Preserved Meats"),
served with toast and chili-flavored oil.

Trutas do Rio Cavado _trootash doo ree-oo kahvahdoo_: (MD)
Whole trout stuffed with lean ham, fried in bacon fat. The
fish is served with boiled potatoes and the diced bacon used
for frying.

THE CENTER EAST

The features of this rustic farming area are reflected in its
food, characterized by the use of local ingredients in the
preparation of its filling dishes, which are always dressed
with first-choice olive oil. Vegetables widely grown in this
part of the country, and many wines, mainly whites and
rosés, are produced and are used in the preparation of
many dishes. The Serra da Estrela, in the south of the
region, home of Serra cheese (see "Cheeses"), has many
specialties based on salted cod. Here are the recipes we
have selected:

Abóbora e beringelas fritas _abohboorah eh behreenjelash
freetash_: (V) Pumpkin and egg plant slices, coated in egg and
breadcrumbs and fried in olive oil.

Almôndegas de lebre _almohndehgash deh lehbreh_: (MD)
Meatballs of minced hare with ham, wine, tomato and eggs.
They are served with rice.

Bacalhau à Assis *bahkalyee<u>ah</u>-oo ah ass<u>ee</u>esh*: (MD) Boneless flesh of salted cod in small pieces browned with onion, carrot, ham and scrambled egg. Served with potatoes.

Bacalhau assado com batatas a murro *bahkalyee<u>ah</u>-oo assah<u>doo</u> kohn bahtah<u>tash</u> ah m<u>oo</u>rroo*: (MD) Thick pieces of salted cod grilled and then put in olive oil flavored with garlic and pepper. Served with potatoes boiled whole in their skins.

Batatas de Caçoilas *baht<u>ah</u>tash deh kass<u>oh</u>-eelash*: (V) Well-cooked potatoes browned in olive oil, with fresh tomatoes and onion. The dish accompanies fried fish.

Grão guisado com ovos *gr<u>ah</u>-oon gees<u>ah</u>doo kohn <u>oh</u>voosh*: (MD) Chickpeas cooked with onion, browned in oil, garlic and mint, then mixed with boiled eggs.

Laburdo *lahb<u>oo</u>rdoo*: (MD) Pig's liver cut into small pieces and cooked in orange juice, lard and wine. It is served on slices of bread with orange segments or slices and rice.

Pastéis de Molho *pahsht<u>eh</u>-eesh deh m<u>oh</u>lyoo*: (S/MD) Puff pastry pie with a filling of mince, covered with a sauce made from vinegar, saffron and parsley.

Perdizes fritas à Outeiro *perd<u>ee</u>sesh fr<u>ee</u>tash ah oh-oot<u>eh</u>-eeroo*: (MD) Fried partridge with a white wine and meat broth sauce cooked in the oil used to fry the birds. Served with fried potatoes.

Salada de coelho bravo *sahl<u>ah</u>dah deh kw<u>eh</u>lyoo br<u>ah</u>voo*: (MD) A salad with wild rabbit's meat in small strips, in a *vinagrete* sauce (see "Gastronomic Terms"). Served with fried potatoes.

Sopa de favas _sohpah deh fahvash_: (S) A soup made from broad beans, potatoes, onions, and coriander. It is served with toast.

Torresmos da Beira _tooreshmoosh dah beh-eerah_: (MD) Pork cutlets and fatty cuts of pork, cut in pieces, marinated in white wine and bay leaves, and fried in lard. Served with boiled potatoes.

THE CENTER WEST

This area is where the capital is located, and also the wonderful places on the Costa da Prata (the Silver Coast), on the Atlantic coast, which heavily influences eating habits in the region. An infinite variety of fish and seafood dishes, nearly always highly spiced, is the basis of local food. Meat, however, also plays an important part, especially in the towns.
Here are some characteristic dishes:

Açorda de mariscos _assordah deh mareeshkoosh_: (S/MD) Bread with oil, garlic and seafood (see "Recipes").

Amêijoas à Bulhão Pato _ahmeh-eejooash ah boolyaoon pahtoo_: (S) Clams cooked in oil, garlic, lemon and pepper, served with lemon.

Arroz de alhos _arrosh deh ahlyoosh_: (V) Rice with a good deal of garlic browned in olive oil. Served to accompany fried fish.

Arroz de grelos or **de brócolis** _arrosh deh grehloosh_ or _deh brohkooleesh_: (V) Rice cooked with grelos, a local vegetable, or with broccoli. Used to accompany fried fish.

Bacalhau à Brás *bahkahlyah-oo ah brash*: (MD) A dish of salted cod, fried potatoes, scrambled eggs, black olives, garlic, and oil.

Bife à Marrare *beefeh ah marahreh*: (MD) A steak in a butter and cream sauce. It is served with fried potatoes and salad.

Caldeirada à pescador *kahldeh-eerahdah ah peskahdor*: (S/MD) A very common type of fish soup, using a wide variety of different fish cooked with onion, garlic, tomato, bread, and potatoes.

Caracóis à portuguesa *karakoh-eesh ah poortoogehza*: (S/V) Snails browned in oil with bay leaves, garlic, onion and chili-flavored oil.

Creme de camarão *krehm de kahmahraoon*: (S/V) A soup made from black prawns, cooked with tomato, white wine, and chili-flavored oil.

Enguias à moda do Ribatejo *engee-ash ah mohdah doo reebahtehjoo*: (MD) Eels cut in pieces and cooked with onion, wine, parsley, vinegar, and oil. The dish is accompanied by rice or mashed potatoes.

Fígado de porco de cebolada *feegahdoo deh porkoo deh sehboolahdah*: (MD) Slices of pig's liver encrusted with garlic and fried with sliced onion. The dish is served with boiled potatoes.

Lagosta suada à moda de Peniche *lahgoshtah sooahdah ah mohdah deh pehneesheh*: (MD) Lobster with white wine, Port wine, and aquavitae, with tomatoes, onion and chili-flavored oil added. It is served with rice.

Pataniscas de bacalhau *pahtahneeshkash deh bakahlyah-oo*: (S) Small pieces of salted cod, skinned and boned, covered in batter and fried in olive oil.

Peixe frito de Escabeche *peh-eesheh freetoh deh shkahbehsheh*: (MD) Swordfish, sardines and other kinds of fish, first fried and then covered with a sauce made from onions, garlic, bay leaves, parsley, oil, vinegar, and pepper.

Sopa de entulho *sohpah deh entoolyoo*: (S) A filling, nutritious soup made from pork, beans and vegetables (potatoes, turnips, and pumpkin).

THE CENTER SOUTH

The Alentejo is the driest part of the country, therefore the food resources do not offer very much. For this reason local people have transformed the usual bread and dried meats into the basic ingredients of regional cookery. Local game and freshwater fish complete the menu, which is, in the end, extremely creative!

Assado de peixe *assahdoo deh peh-eesheh*: (MD) Grilled freshwater fish with a chili-flavored sauce, vinegar, oil, and garlic. The dish is served with either boiled or fried potatoes.

Carneiro assado *karneh-eeroo assahdoo*: (MD) A sheep's foot marinated in white wine and garlic, then roasted. It is accompanied by fried potatoes and lettuce.

Empadas de galinha *ehmpahdash deh gahleenyah*: (S) A chicken pie also containing bacon, pepper and lemon.

Espargos bravos com ovos *shpargoosh brahvoosh kohn ohvoosh*: (V) Asparagus cooked with fresh breadcrumb and egg yolk.

Feijão branco com cabeça de porco *feh-eejaoon brahnkoo kohn kahbehsah deh porkoo*: (MD) White beans cooked with the local sausage and pig's head.

Feijão verde à Alentejana *feh-eejaoon verdeh ah ahlehntejahnah*: Green beans cooked with potatoes, carrots, tomato, garlic, and sausage.

Migas à Alentejana *meegash ah ahlentehjahnah*: (MD) A dish of fried pork, bread and cream of peppers.

Miolos *myohloosh*: (MD) Ox brain cooked with bacon, bread, a cream made from bell peppers, garlic and oil

Sarapatel *sarahpahtehl*: (MD) Baby goat or piglet tripe, cooked with blood, white wine, bacon, bread, onion, and various spices.

Sopa à Alentejana *sohpah ah ahlentehjahnah*: (S) A soup made using coriander, garlic browned in olive oil, bread and eggs. It is often used to accompany grilled sardines.

REGIONAL DISHES

THE SOUTH

This is the Algarve, the southern coastline, temperate in climate and rich in natural beauty. The wholesome, tasty local food is mainly based on fish and seafood accompanied by salads and cool wine.

Amêijoas na Cataplana *ahmeh-eejooash nah kahtahplahnah*: (S) Clams cooked with onion, lean ham, chili-flavored oil and parsley.

Arroz de polvo *arosh deh pohlvoo*: (MD) Rice cooked with octopus in white wine and oil flavored with chili.

Bifes de atum em cebolada *beefesh deh ahtoon ehn sehboolahdah*: (MD) Slices of fresh tunafish fried in oil, with generous amounts onion and garlic. Served with potatoes.

Cozido de grão *koozeedoo deh graoon*: (MD) Beef, sausage, chickpeas and vegetables (pumpkin and green beans) all cooked in the same water. This is served with rice.

Estopeta de atum *shtoopehtah deh ahtoon*: (MD) Fresh tunafish done with tomatoes, bell peppers and onions.

Lulas cheias *loolash sheh-eeash*: (S/MD) Cuttlefish stuffed with rice, ham and tomato.

Lulas com ferrado *loolash kohn ferahdoo*: (MD) Cuttlefish browned whole (with their black liquid) in garlic and oil.

Sopa de cabeça de peixe *sohpah deh kahbessah deh peh-eesheh*: (S) A soup made from fish heads, potatoes, tomatoes, eggs, and chili-flavored oil.

REGIONAL DISHES

MADEIRA

Madeira is considered a piece of paradise: a place of
wonderful scenery and splendid colors, where life goes on as
it did in bygone times, healthy and calm. Although the main
activity of the island is fishing, local cookery also contains a
good deal of meat. Thanks to its geographical position,
tropical fruit and other exotic products are available.
The following is our choice for you:

Atum assado *ahtoon assahdoo*: (MD) Pieces of tunafish
marinated then grilled, accompanied by potatoes, tiny
pickled onions and maize.

Bacalhau de São Martinho *bahkahlyah-oo deh saoon
marteenyoo*: (MD) Salted cod grilled and *flambé* with
aquavitae, then dressed with garlic, oil and vinegar.

Brodo de carne *brohdoo deh karneh*: (S) Beef on the bone
cooked in broth with onion, tomato, turnip and very thin
strips of pasta.

Carne de vinha d'alhos *karneh deh veenyah dahlyoosh*:
(MD) Loin of pork marinated with wine and garlic and served
with bread (see "Recipes").

Milho frito *meelyoo freetoo*: (V) Corn flour, cabbage, and
butter worked into a kind of batter, diced, then fried.

REGIONAL DISHES

THE AZORES

This archipelago is made up of nine islands, some of which are rather wild. The inhabitants, the *Açorianos*, work hard in the fields and devote the same energy to fishing. The food, obviously, is mainly fish, but also includes some preserved meats treated in the same way as on the mainland.

Arroz de lapas *arosh deh lahpash*: (MD) Rice with shellfish done with onion, bay leaves and parsley.

Canarinhos *kahnareenyoosh*: (S/MD) Fried canaries dressed with garlic, oil with chili, white wine, vinegar, and oil.

Carne de ganso à antiga *karneh deh gahnsoo ah anteegah*: (MD) Wild goose cooked with tomato, onion, cinnamon, bay leaves and chili-flavored oil. Served with roast potatoes.

Polvo guisado *pohlvoo geesahdoo*: (MD) Octopus cooked with pepper, chili-flavored oil, white wine and Port wine, parsley, garlic, and lard. Served with boiled potatoes.

BRAZIL

THE NORTH

This region, occupying roughly half the total area of the country and including Amazonia, is one of the most undeveloped in the nation and is also where the native inhabitants' influence is still most strongly felt. Local food is decidedly exotic and quite different from that found elsewhere in Brazil; however, if you are not feeling adventurous – seeing that it is an area of fascinating tourist attractions – you will also find a number of culinary options which are more "familiar."

Casquinha de Siri *kashkeenyah djee seeree*: (S) A dish of the large crabs which are typical of this region (see "National Dishes").

Jacaré *jahkareh*: (MD) The *jacaré* is a small crocodile; its meat is very tasty, and is cut into steaks and fried in oil with garlic, onion, and tomatoes.

Pombos *pohnboosh*: (MD) Pigeons either roast or cooked with coconut milk.

Tartaruga *tartaroogah*: (MD) Turtle dishes, which are considered great delicacies in other parts of the world, are considered more or less normal here. The meat of small turtles (*muçua*) is on sale in the markets, already cleaned and cut. It is cooked as a steak with salt, garlic, and lemon, or as a casserole or in soups. The fragrance of turtle dishes is one of its features.

REGIONAL DISHES

THE NORTH EAST

This region, the most densely populated of the country, furnishes some delicious ingredients like *dendê* oil and the *de sol* meat (see "Other Specialties"). With its beaches and marvelous sea, the North East is the part most frequently explored by tourists, especially in the last few years. Local food features mainly seafood. Furthermore, this region offers the opportunity of tasting exotic tropical fruit juices like *guaranà* and cocoa.

Here are some of the most typical dishes:

Angu de arroz nordestino *angoo djee arosh nordeshteenoo*: (V) A dish of maize flour cooked with coconut milk and rice flour.

Arroz de côco *arosh djee kohkoo*: (V) Rice cooked in coconut milk.

Camarão com côco *kahmahraoon kohn kohkoo*: (MD) Prawns cooked in coconut milk with a sauce made from onion, tomato, and garlic (see "Recipes").

Casquinhos de lagosta *kashkeenyoosh djee lahgoshtah*: (MD) Lobster prepared with potatoes, butter, onion and milk and served in its shell.

Peixe frito *peh-eeshee freetoo*: (MD) Pieces of fish marinated in lemon, garlic, salt and pepper, dipped in manioca flour and then fried in oil.

Sopa de macaxeira *sohpah djee makasheh-eerah*: (S) A soup made from a local root called *aipim*.

Vatapá do nordeste *vahtahpah doo nordeshtee*: (MD) A dish made from dried prawns, fresh fish, ginger, coconut milk, chestnuts and rice flour. It is eaten with *angu*.

THE BAHIA REGION

Even though geographically speaking this area is part of the North East, we are describing it separately because of its highly individual gastronomic character. In Bahia nearly all dishes contain a touch of oil strongly flavored with chili and of *azeite de dendê*, a dark orange oil extracted from palms. Should you not like these flavors, it would be well to advise the waiter of the fact before ordering your meal!
The following is a description of some of the typical dishes.

Abóbora com camarão seco *ahbohbohrah kohn kahmahraoon sehkoo*: (MD) Pumpkin cooked with dried prawns, tomatoes, garlic, coriander, *dendê* oil and eggs.

Acarajé *ahkahrahjeh*: (V) Croquettes made from black beans and fried dried prawns, stewed in *dendê* oil. They are sold in the streets by the "baianas," women in the traditional white costume of the region.

Bobó de camarão *bohboh djee kahmahraoon*: (MD) The most popular dish of the region, made from large prawns fried in butter with garlic, tomato, chili-flavored oil, and other ingredients, with the addition of cooked manioca and coconut milk. This food is served with rice.

Carne seca com jerimum *karneh sehkah kohn jehreemoom*: (MD) Dried meat (see "Other Specialties") fried with pumpkin, onion, garlic, and pepper.

Caruru *kahrooroo*: (MD) Highly spiced dish made from *quiabos*, a local vegetable, stewed with dried prawns with toasted peanuts added as a final touch.

Molho de camarão *mohlyoo djee kahmaraoon*: (V) A sauce made from prawns cooked with coconut milk, chili and Maizena flour. It is used with various types of fish, or on boiled rice.

Moqueca de peixe *mookehkah djee peh-eeshee*: (MD) Fish cooked with coriander, onion, garlic, tomatoes, peanuts, and other ingredients. The liquid left over from cooking the fish is used to make *pirão* (see below).

Pirão *peeraoon*: (V) A dish made from manioca flour, used to accompany *moqueca de peixe* (see above).

Vatapá *vahtahpah*: (MD) This is a spicier version of the *vatapá* of the North East (see above), made with salted cod and other fish.

Xinxim de galinha *sheensheen djee gahleenah*: (MD) Chicken stewed with dried prawns and other ingredients (see "Recipes").

THE CENTER WEST

Meat consumption is high in this area, both because of the number of *fazendas* raising beef, and because the Pantanal region has a wide variety of game. Rice is another staple of production and consumption here, while fish abound in the great Araguaia River which flows into the Amazon. Along the banks, there are many comfortable hotels near local native communities.

A further feature of this area's food is the plentiful use of ginger, saffron and pepper. International cuisine is available in the capital, Brasília.

Angu goiano *ahngoo goyahnoo*: (V) A kind of porridge made from green maize cobs. It is served with *quiabos* (a local vegetable) and with chicken prepared with ginger and pepper.

Arroz com guariroba *arosh kohn gwareerohbah*: (V) *Guariroba* is a bitter coconut with which this rice dish is cooked.

Arroz do povo *arosh doo pohvoo*: (MD) Rice cooked with slices of meat, garlic, onion, and cooked beans.

Paca *pahkah*: (MD) Paca meat, similar to pork, is roasted with bacon, garlic, onion, pepper, and lemon, and served with rice.

Peixe à Mato Grosso *peh-eeshee ah mahtoo grohsoo*: (MD) Fish wrapped in banana leaves and roasted.

Perdiz *perdeesh*: (MD) Partridge with garlic, bay leaves, pepper, and lemon, and cooked in the oven with butter and a little milk.

REGIONAL DISHES

THE ESPÍRITO SANTO REGION

The food in this area, known as *capixaba*, may well be considered typical of Brazil for the reason that colonization has not made itself felt so much here, at least from the culinary point of view. The dishes, therefore, are examples of cookery created purely by the local population.

Feijão com peixe *feh-eeja̱oon kohn pe̱h-eeshee*: (MD) Black beans cooked and flavored with onion, garlic and bacon with the addition of tomato, oil and fish fillets. Served with rice and chili-flavored oil.

Fritada de carne *freeta̱hdah djee ka̱rnee*: Meat and sausages minced and fried together with eggs and grated cheese.

Muma de siri *mo̱omah djee seere̱e*: (MD) Small crabs cooked with onion, liquid pepper, tomato and *urucu* fat. A thick mixture is obtained by adding manioca flour.

Peixe à moda capixaba *pe̱h-eeshee ah mo̱hdah kahpeesha̱hbah*: (MD) Pieces of fish marinated with various spices and then cooked.

Pitu con côco *peeto̱o kohn ko̱hkooh*: (MD) The *pitù* is a freshwater lobster, marinated and cooked with pieces of coconut. It is served with rice and beans.

THE MINAS GERAIS REGION

The food in Minas Gerais is considered the most simple and genuine; and indeed it does have a wonderful flavor. Local cookery uses a great deal of vegetables, beans, and chicken.

Furthermore, this region is the most important producer of cheese of the country.

Aipim frito *aeepeen freetoo*: (V) *Aipim* is a local root vegetable which is sliced and fried. It is used to accompany a main dish, hot and crisp.

Arroz mineiro *arosh meeneh-eeroo*: (MD) Rice cooked with minced meat, carrots and little potatoes.

Couve à mineira *koh-ooveh ah meeneh-eerah*: (V) Green cabbage sliced very finely then fried with diced bacon. It is eaten with a main dish, or in *feijoada*.

Feijão-manteiga *feh-eejaoon-mahnteh-eegah*: (V) Butterbeans are very soft beans which are cooked and browned in butter and parsley. The dish is served with rice.

Frango com catupiry *frahngoo kohn kahtoopeeree*: (MD) Slithers of chicken browned in pork fat with pieces of *palmito* (see "Other Specialties") and *catupiry* cheese (see "Cheeses").

Frango com creme de milho *frahngoo kohn krehmeh djee meelyoo*: (MD) Chicken cooked with a number of spices and a cream made from maize. Served with rice.

Leitão assado *leh-eetaoon asahdoo*: (MD) Roast suckling pig stuffed with olives and dressed with vinegar, pepper, bay, onion and ham.

Lentilhas à moda de Minas *lehnteelyash ah mohdah djee meenash*: (V/MD) Lentils cooked with garlic, onion and tomatoes, with eggs cooked together with the lentils themselves.

Quiabo com carne moída *kee-ahboo kohn karneh moo-eedah*: (V) A local vegetable with a rather bitter taste, fried with minced meat, garlic and onion.

Quibebe *keebehbeh*: (V) A purée of pumpkin, fried in oil with onion, parsley, marjoram, and meat broth. It is served together with dried meat (see *carne di sol* in "Other Specialties") and rice.

Tutu mineiro *tootoo meeneh-eeroo*: (V/MD) Black beans and bacon mixed with manioca flour (see "Recipes").

THE RIO DE JANEIRO REGION

The food of the *Cidade Maravilhosa*, as the city of Rio de Janeiro is called, is fairly substantial in spite of the climate. Local cooking favors risotto, meat and beans, although salads are also popular. The city boasts a good number of restaurants, among which many are international and Portuguese.
Here is a selection of the best-loved dishes:

Arroz à grega *arosh ah grehgah*: (V) Rice with peas and carrots, bell peppers, and cooked ham in small pieces. This accompanies meat dishes.

Arroz com feijão *arosh kohn feh-eejaoon*: For most *cariocas* (the inhabitants of Rio), this combination of rice and black beans is an essential dish in everyday cooking, to accompany both meat and fish.

Batata sotê *bahtahtah soteh*: (V) Boiled potatoes cut into pieces, browned in butter and sprinkled with parsley. To be served with steak.

Bife / Filé *beefeh / feeleh*: (MD) Beef, pork or even chicken steaks or fillet steaks are served almost daily in this part of the world. Steak is served in many different ways, for example fried in egg and breadcrumbs or *à cavalo* (see "Gastronomic Terms") or else done with a variety of sauces. It is almost always accompanied by fried potatoes and salad.

Churrasco *shoorashkoo*: (MD) Roast meat is very popular, and there are many restaurants, the *churrascarias,* where at least ten kinds of roast meat together with dozens of different side dishes are served in the form of *rodizio,* or at a fixed price.

Farofa *fahrohfah*: (V) Manioca flour toasted in butter and salt, to which a number of other ingredients may be added: diced bacon, eggs or even pieces of fruit. This is a very popular side dish to go with steaks and even feijoada.

Feijoada *feh-eejooahdah*: (MD) This is the most famous dish of the region, nutritious and filling. It is made of black beans cooked with pork and other ingredients (see "Recipes").

Picadinho de carne *peekahdjeenyoo djee karnee*: (MD) A stew cooked with onion and meat broth. It is served with rice.

Rodízio de massas *rohdeezyoo djee mahsash*: (MD) A number of different shapes and sizes of pasta are served together in one dish.

Salpicão *sahlpeekaoon*: (S/V) This is a kind of mixed salad, fairly simple but also used on special occasions. It is a mixture of slithers of chicken breast, potatoes, *palmito* (see "Other Specialties"), maize, asparagus, peas, apples and other ingredients bound together with mayonnaise and cream.

REGIONAL DISHES

Sopa de ervilhas _sohpah djee erveelyash_: (V) Pea soup made with bacon, onion and tomato. Served with toast.

Torta salgada _tortah salgahdah_: (S/MD) Savory pies are very popular. They can have a variety of fillings: chicken, ricotta cheese, ham, tomato, eggs, _palmito_ (see "Other Specialties").

THE SÃO PAULO REGION

São Paulo, the largest city in Latin America, is a highly developed international metropolis, always on the move. It has the most cosmopolitan food of the nation, with features of Portuguese, Spanish, Arab, German, Italian, and Eastern cookery. Some of the dishes we list here are, therefore, of foreign origin, although they are now an integral part of local eating habits.

Almôndegas _ahlmohndehgash_: (MD) Meatballs, bacon, and sausages fried then served in tomato sauce, together with rice or spaghetti.

Camarões à paulista _kahmahroh-eensh ah pah-ooleeshtah_: (V/MD) Large prawns marinated in lemon juice, garlic, salt, vinegar, and spring onion, then fried in oil.

Cuscuz à paulista _kooshkoosh ah pah-ooleeshtah_: (V/MD) Maize flour cooked with tomatoes, cabbage, bell peppers, small pieces of chicken, cooked eggs and _palmito_ (see "Other Specialties"). Being very filling, it is often served as a complete meal.

Inhoque com carne assada _eenyohkeh kohn karneh assahdah_: (MD) Small soft potato-and-flour balls (similar to

Italian *gnocchi*) cooked in water then served with tomato sauce with slices of roast meat.

Quibe _keebeh_: (S/V) A meat loaf made of minced meat with mint and flour, served with lemon juice.

Turlu-furnu *toorloo foornoo:* (V) Egg plant, potatoes, courgettes, onions, and tomatoes sliced and baked in the oven, with bread and grated cheese.

Viradinho à paulista *veerahdjeenyoo ah pah-ooleeshtah:* (MD) *Mulatinho* beans cooked with diced bacon, onion, garlic, and maize flour. They are served with fried sausages, rice and one single egg.

THE SOUTH

The South is a unique and fascinating place. It almost seems to be a separate country within Brazil itself, seeing that the climate, the appearance of the people, and their customs regarding life in general and food in particular are more European than Latin American. Their cooking is rich, the prevalent features being beef and game. And this is also the greatest coffee-exporting region, as well as being the area where traditional German and Italian methods are used in the local production of wines and beers.

These southern dishes are to be found all over the country:

Arroz de carreteiro *arosh djee karehteh-eeroo*: (V) Risotto made with a particular type of meat called *charque* fried with onions and tomatoes.

Chimarrão *sheemaraoon:* a particular kind of tea with a very strong flavor, from a plant called *mate*; it is filtered very slowly through a special container and then drunk while still very hot.

Churrasco à Gaúcha *shoorashkoo ah gah-ooshah*: (MD) The custom of grilling meat comes from this area. During cooking, the meats are basted every now and then with pickled herbs.

Coelho assado *koo-ehlyoo assahdoo*: (MD) Rabbit marinated in white wine, garlic, onion, and bay, then roast with bacon.

Frango à caipira *frahngoo ah kah-eepeerah*: (MD) Risotto made with chicken pieces, bell peppers, and onions, all put in the oven to brown with cheese.

Galeto *gahlehtoo*: (S/MD) Small cockerel cut in pieces, salted and peppered and sprinkled with lemon, then grilled. Around Rio, the dish is accompanied by fried potatoes, while in the South it is served with a maize porridge.

Lombinho *lohnbeenyoo*: (MD) Loin of pork with a sauce made of various ingredients (see "Recipes").

Pastelão de Vila Velha *pashtehlaoon djee veelah vehlyah*: (S/MD) A kind of pudding made of flour, lard, milk, and eggs, containing a sauce of prawns and palmito (see "Other Specialties").

Puchero do Paraná *pooshehroo doo pahrahnah*: (MD) Beef cooked with onion, garlic, tomatoes, and bell peppers. When cooked, sausages, potatoes, carrots, pumpkin, spinach and bananas are added.

Sopa de beterraba or **de milho verde** _sohpah djee behtehrahbah_ or _djee meelyoo vehrdjee_: (S) A soup made from egg plant (see "Recipes") or of green maize cobs.

Strogonoff à moda do Paraná _strohgohnohf ah mohdah doo pahrahnah_: (MD) Fillet browned in garlic and butter, with a sauce of mushroom, cream, and tomato. It is accompanied by rice or roast potatoes.

RECIPES

The quantities given are for four people.

🍴 (P) Açorda de camarão

Medium-sized shelled prawns	*500 g*	*(1 lb)*
Stale bread	*500 g*	*(1 lb)*
3 cloves of garlic		
3 spoons of olive oil		
Fish broth	*100 ml*	*(3 fl. oz)*
3 or 4 egg yolks		
Salt, pepper, chili		

Cook the prawns in very little water flavored with parsley and white wine. Soak the bread in the cooking water from the prawns and add it to the pan in which you are frying the chopped garlic in oil. Add the fish broth and mix with a wooden spoon until it boils. Add salt, pepper and chili. Add the prawns, leaving aside a few for the final decoration, mix and remove pan from heat. Add the yolks, mixing immediately to avoid lumps. Decorate the dish with the remaining prawns and parsley. Serve with chilled white wine.
Açorda can be made with lobster, clams, or salted cod instead of prawns.

(P) Arroz de cabidela

1 fresh chicken with its blood in a sachet
2 medium-sized onions
Rice, well washed and dried   400 g   (14 oz)
4 spoons of olive oil
1 clove of garlic
1 bunch of parsley
½ glass of vinegar
Bay leaf, salt and pepper

Mix the blood and vinegar together keeping them liquid. Cut the chicken into pieces and brown with the oil, onions, garlic and parsley. When the liquid has evaporated, add a little water, the salt and pepper, and leave to cook slowly. When the meat is nearly cooked, add the water necessary to cook the rice (at least three times the volume of the rice so that it will not boil dry). When the water boils, add the rice. When it is cooked add the blood, mixing until boiling point is reached then immediately remove from the heat. This dish must be served very hot, accompanied by red wine.

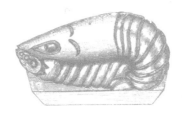

(B) Babá-de-moça

Sugar	*200 g*	*(7 oz)*
8 egg yolks		
Coconut milk	*approx. 1 liter*	*(2 pt)*

Mix the sugar with about 1½ cups of water and cook over a low heat until the mixture becomes firm. Remove from heat and allow to cool. In the meantime, mix the yolks with the coconut milk and add this to the dense sugar. Heat again mixing well, then allow to cool. The cream can then be eaten by itself, or on a pudding, or as a cake filling.

(P) BACALHAU À ZÉ DO PIPO

Thick slices of salted cod, skinned and boned	400 g	(14 oz)
Fresh milk	1 liter	(2 pt)
2 medium-sized onions		
4 spoons of olive oil		
1 cup of mayonnaise		
Mashed potatoes	Approx. 750 g.	(1 ½ lb)
Bay leaf, salt and pepper		

Cook the fish in the milk. When it is done remove from the liquid and place in an earthenware pot. Meantime cook the sliced onion without browning in oil with salt, pepper and a little of the milk in which the fish was cooked. Cover the slices of cod with the onion and then with mayonnaise. Cover the whole with mashed potato and put in the oven to brown. When it is ready, decorate with tasty black olives. The dish should by accompanied by red or rosé wine.

(P) BIFES DE ATUM COM TOMATE

Thick slices of fresh tunafish	*800 g*	*(1 ½ lb)*
Fresh tomatoes	*500 g*	*(1 lb)*
3 onions		
2 cloves of garlic		
3 spoons of olive oil		
Bay leaves, salt and pepper		

Slice onions and tomatoes. Place half in a pan and lay the fish slices on top with the bay leaves, salt and pepper. Cover this layer with the rest of the sliced onions and tomatoes and pour on the oil. Cook slowly, with the pan convered until halfway through. Uncover and leave to cook, making sure the sauce does not boil dry. Serve with chips or salad, with a cool white wine.

(P) Cabrito assado

1 kid goat's foot
Potatoes   1 kg   (2 lb)
4 cloves of garlic
2 onions
3 spoons of lard
1 bunch of parsley
1 glass of white wine
1 spoon of creamed bell peppers
Salt, pepper, bay leaf, and saffron

Crush the garlic together with half the parsley and the salt.
Cover the meat with this mixture then cover with the sliced
onion, the lard, the bay leaf, pepper, the creamed bell
peppers and the saffron. Add some more parsley, the white
wine and a little water, and place the potatoes around. Put in
the oven until perfectly cooked. Serve with green salad.

(B) Camarão com côco

Fresh prawns	1 kg	(2 lb)

1 spoon of vinegar
2 spoons of oil of dendê
2 cloves of garlic
2 egg yolks
1 onion
Juice of 1 lemon
Milk from 2 coconuts
Salt, spring onion

Clean the prawns well, and cook in salted water with the lemon juice. When cooked, remove the heads and mince them with a little water to make a paste. In a saucepan, combine the coconut milk, the paste made from the heads, the chopped onion and garlic, the skinned tomatoes, the spring onion, the oil, the vinegar, and the egg yolk. Mix well. Bring to the boil slowly, mixing well, add the prawns and continue mixing till cooked. Add salt if necessary. Serve with rice, or fried bean croquettes.

(P) Carne de vinha-d'alhos

Pork	600 g	~ (1 ⅓ lb)
8 thick (½ in/1.5 cm) slices of bread		
Small potatoes	300 g	(11 oz)
Sweet potatoes	300 g	(11 oz)
2 or 3 glasses of white wine		
1 glass of vinegar		
6 cloves of garlic		
Salt, pepper, and chili		
Slices of orange and lemon		

Rinse the meat in warm water and cut into small pieces. Leave it to marinate in a mixture of wine, vinegar, garlic, salt and pepper for at least 2 or 3 days in the lower part of the fridge. Cook the meat in the marinade; while it is cooking, let the slices of bread absorb some of the sauce without letting them crumble. When the meat is almost cooked, remove it from the heat and let it cool. When it is cold, use the fat which forms on top of it to fry both the pieces of pork and the slices of bread (should the fat be too little, add some oil). In the meantime cook the potatoes and brown them in the same fat in which the meat was fried.

Finally, carefully place the bread slices in a large dish, then on top place the meat, and on the meat a few slices of orange and lemon. The potatoes can be decorated with cooked baby onions.

RECISES

 (B) Creme de abacaxi

1 large, ripe pineapple
Grated coconut   200 g   (7 oz)
Milk   1 liter   (2 pt)
4 spoons of sugar
1 spoon of Maizena flour
1 teaspoon of vanilla

Peel the pineapple and remove the hard central core. Cut the
fruit into small pieces and put these onto a plate, covering
them with the grated coconut. Cook the other ingredients
very slowly to make a cream with which to cover the
pineapple.
This sweet should be kept in the fridge for at least two or
three hours before being served. Decorate with whipped
cream.

(B) FEIJOADA À CARIOCA

Choice black beans	1 kg	(2 lb)
Different meats	1 kg	(2 lb)

(e.g. 500g (1 lb) each of dried beef,
   and pork; a pig's trotter and ear)
1 pig's tongue
1 spoon of lard
1 large onion
3 or 4 cloves of garlic

Put the beans and the meat salted in water for 24 hours.
Rinse the meat and cook it together with the beans and the
tongue in plenty of water (in a pressure cooker, the cooking
time will be about 25 minutes). In the meantime, fry together
the lard, the onion and the garlic. Add a cup of cooked
beans to the frying pan, crushing them well. Mix and add to
the other beans and the cooked meats. Replace over the heat
and finish cooking slowly. Check the salt.
Serve with rice, manioc flour, green cabbage à *mineira*
(sliced finely and browned with bacon), peeled and cut
oranges and oil flavored with chili.
Before the meal, you might enjoy a *caipirinha*, and cool beer
with the food.

RECIPES

 (P) Gaspacho à alentejana

4 ripe tomatoes
1 green bell pepper
1 cucumber
3 cloves of garlic
3 spoons of olive oil
4 spoons of vinegar
Stale bread   200 g   (7 oz)
A spoon and a half of salt

Crush the garlic with the salt, then add the oil and vinegar.
Purée two of the tomatoes and add that to the mixture. Cut
the other two tomatoes, the bell pepper, and the cucumber
into pieces and put them into a soup tureen together with the
garlic and tomato purée, and about one and a half liters
(about three pints) of chilled water. Just before serving, add
the diced bread. This soup should always be served chilled,
if possible with ham and small sausages.

(P) LEITE-CREME

Milk	*1 liter*	*(2 pt)*
5 spoons of sugar		
5 egg yolks		
1 spoon of flour		
Lemon rind		

Thoroughly blend the egg yolks with the sugar and flour. Add the boiling milk and lemon rind. Bring to the boil, stirring continuously. When the cream is ready, put it into the serving dish and burn a little sugar on the top. The sweet should be served warm.

RECIPES

 (B) LOMBINHO DE PORCO RECHEADO

Loin of pork	*1 kg*	*(2 lb)*
Diced ham	*100 g*	*(4 oz)*
1 egg yolk		
1 small onion		
1 spoon of tomato purée		
1 cup fresh breadcrumbs		
1 cup of diced apple		
Salt, pepper, bay leaves, lemon		

The loin of pork should be sliced but without actually separating the pieces one from another. Sprinkle with salt, pepper, and lemon juice and add the bay, leaving the meat to marinate for at least two hours. Mix the apple with the bread, the grated lemon rind, the tomato purée, the finely chopped onion, and the ham. Put a little of this mixture between the slices, then tie the meat up to form a single joint.

Roast in the oven. Serve with *farofa* (see Regional Dishes), fried bananas and rice.

(B) Moqueca de peixe

| Fish fillets | 1 kg | (2 lb) |

2 or 3 onions
3 or 4 fresh tomatoes
Juice of one lemon
Coriander, salt, pepper
A little oil (preferably of dendê)
Manioca flour

Crush the coriander and mix it with the onions, the tomatoes and pepper (green bell peppers, peanuts and various spices may also be used). Cover the fish fillets with this cream. Add salt and lemon juice.
Put on a low heat, add a little water and oil and cook until the fish is tender. Add enough manioca flour to the liquid that is left to obtain a thick cream. The dish is served with rice.

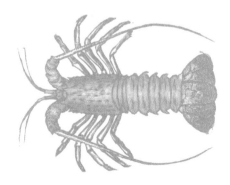

🍴 (B) Pavê de pêssego

Milk	*1 liter*	*(2 pt)*

1 can of peaches in syrup
6 spoons of sugar
1 spoon of Maizena flour
3 egg yolks
1 lemon or 1 teaspoon of vanilla
Sweet biscuits
A little liqueur-like wine

Soften the biscuits in the wine. On a low heat, make a custard cream with the milk, 4 spoons of sugar and the egg yolks already mixed with the other part of sugar. When this is ready, add the grated lemon rind or the vanilla and let it cool.
In a deep rectangular dish, put in a layer of the custard cream, one of biscuits, then one of peach pieces. Continue forming these layers until the ingredients are finished; the top layer should be peaches. If desired, decorate with whipped cream. Serve chilled well.

(P) Queijadas de Sintra

3 large cups of flour
1 spoon of butter or margarine
Fresh, unsalted cheese
4 egg yolks
2 cups of sugar
Cinnamon, salt, and water

Make a dough with two cups of flour, the melted butter and a little water, slightly salted. This dough must be left to rise for about 24 hours and should become fairly hard. Grate the cheese and mix it with the sugar. Add the egg yolks, the rest of the flour and the cinnamon, and beat until the mixture is smooth.
Roll out the dough prepared the day before, and cut it into circular shapes of about two and a half or 3 inches, (6 centimeters) in diameter. Cover each shape with the cheese cream, fold and seal them and bake in the oven for about 15 minutes.

(P) Rojões à moda do Minho

Meat from pig's trotter (skinless but with fat)	800 g	(1 ¾ lb)
Tripe or gut	300 g	(11 oz)
Loin of pork	300 g	(11 oz)
Pig's liver	100 g	(4 oz)

1 glass of cooked pig's blood
3 glasses of new white wine
3 spoons of lard
4 cloves of garlic
20 roasted chestnuts (peeled)
Bay, salt and pepper

Cut the pork meat into pieces, and marinate it for about two hours in the wine, crushed garlic, salt, pepper and bay. Put the meat and the liquid in a pan and cook briskly to evaporate the wine. Add the lard and cook slowly until the meat is brown. At this point, remove some of the fat from the pan and, in a separate pan, use it to fry first the tripe, then the loin, the liver and the blood, all cut into small pieces. Then add everything to the cooked pig's trotter, and the chestnuts. The dish should be served with lemon juice, and with roasted potatoes.

(B) Sopa de beterraba

Pork cutlets	200 g	(7 oz)
2 beetroots		
1 medium-sized potato		
1 carrot, 1 onion, 1 cabbage		
3 or 4 ripe tomatoes		
Oil		

Fry the cut onion and tomatoes in the oil. Add about 1 liter (2 pints) of water and the pork, and leave to cook well. When cooked, take out the meat and set it aside; cut the potato, carrot, cabbage and beetroot into small pieces and put them into the broth. Check the salt. When the vegetables are cooked, remove them from the broth. If desired the soup may be thickened by adding a little flour dissolved in water. Serve the broth, adding some vegetables and a cutlet to each plate.

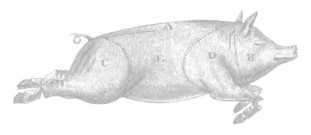

(B) TUTU À MINEIRA

Loin of pork, sliced, or small fried sausages
as many as are necessary (for 4 people)

Bacon	*200 g*	*(7 oz)*
Black beans	*400 g*	*(14 oz)*

1 onion
3 or 4 cloves of garlic
4 eggs
Manioca flour
Salt and pepper

Fry the diced bacon until crisp. In another pan, using the bacon fat, fry the chopped onion and garlic and add the cooked beans. Add salt and pepper. Sprinkle the manioca flour onto the beans until the mixture is of the consistency of a thick cream. Place the *tutu* in the middle of a large serving dish with the bacon pieces on it and the meat around it. Serve with rice, a fried egg each, and boiled chicory browned in oil with garlic.

(B) Xinxim de galinha

1 fresh chicken
1 glass of dried prawns
Toasted peanuts, crushed 100 g (4 oz)
1 onion
3 or 4 cloves of garlic
Juice of one lemon
Oil of dendê
Salt, chili, and parsley

Clean the chicken and cut into pieces. Spread with crushed garlic, lemon juice and salt. Fry the chopped onion, the dried prawns, the peanuts, the chili, and the parsley in the *dendê* oil. Add the chicken pieces and cook, adding a little water when necessary. Serve with rice.

The Portuguese alphabet contains twenty-three letters. In the following table you will see each letter together with its pronunciation in italics, and the word generally used to indicate it when spelling:

a	*ah*	de **amor**	*am<u>o</u>r*
b	*beh*	de **Brasil**	*braz<u>ee</u>l*
c	*seh*	de **casa**	*<u>ka</u>hzah*
d	*deh*	de **dado**	*<u>da</u>hdoo*
e	*eh*	de **elefante**	*elef<u>a</u>hnteh*
f	*<u>eh</u>feh*	de **faca**	*<u>fa</u>hkah*
g	*djeh*	de **girafa**	*djeer<u>a</u>hfah*
h	*a<u>ga</u>h*	de **hotel**	*hotel*
i	*ee*	de **igreja**	*eegr<u>eh</u>jah*
j	*<u>jo</u>htah*	de **janela**	*jan<u>eh</u>lah*
	(as in English *plea<u>s</u>ure*)		
l	*<u>eh</u>leh*	de **leão**	*leh-<u>aoon</u>*
m	*<u>eh</u>me*	de **Maria**	*mahr<u>ee</u>ah*
n	*<u>eh</u>ne*	de **nariz**	*nahr<u>ee</u>sh*
o	*oh*	de **ódio**	*<u>oh</u>dee-oo*
p	*peh*	de **Porto**	*P<u>o</u>rtoo*
q	*keh*	de **quase**	*<u>ka</u>hseh*
r	*<u>eh</u>reh*	de **raiz**	*r<u>ah</u>-eesh*
s	*<u>eh</u>sseh*	de **sapo**	*<u>sa</u>hpoo*
t	*teh*	de **tanto**	*<u>ta</u>hntoo*
u	*oo*	de **união**	*oonee-<u>ahoon</u>*
v	*veh*	de **vício**	*v<u>ee</u>seeoo*
x	*shees*	de **xarope**	*shah<u>ro</u>hpeh*
z	*zeh*	de **zoológico**	*zohl<u>oh</u>dgeekoo*

LETTERS FOUND ONLY IN ABBREVIATIONS AND IN FOREIGN WORDS:

k	*kappa*	w	*<u>da</u>hblyoo*	y	*<u>ee</u>psehlohn*

See also the section on **Pronunciation**.

Are there reduced prices for children?	**Fazem reduções(P) descontos(B) para as crianças?** *fahzen rehdoossoh-eensh (P) deshkohntoosh (B) pahrah ash kree-ahnsash?*
Do you have a cot for the baby?	**Vocês têm um berço para o bebê?** *vossesh teh-eem oon bersoo pahrah oo behbeh?*
Do you have a menu for children?	**Vocês têm um menu para as crianças?** *vossesh teh-eem oon mehnoo pahrah ash kree-ahnsash?*
Have you got a high chair?	**Vocês têm uma cadeirinha?** *vossesh teh-eem oomah kadeh-eereenyah?*
Where can I feed /	**Aonde posso amamentar/trocar as fraldas change the baby? do bebê?** *ah-ohndeh pohssoo ahmahmentar / trookar ash frahldash doo behbeh?*
Where can I find some toy shops?	**Aonde são as lojas de brinquedos?** *ah-ohndeh saoon ash lohjash deh breenkehdoosh?*
I have a small child / two children	**Tenho uma / duas crianças** *tehnyoo ooma / doo-ash kree-ahnsash*
Can you heat the bottle?	**Pode-me aquecer(P) Me pode esquentar(B) o bibéron?** *pohdeh-meh akeser (P) Mee pohdeh eeskehntar (B) oo beebehrohn?*

| There is too much noise here | **Aqui tem muito barulho** |
| | *ahkee tehn moo-eentoo baroolyoo* |

| There is too much smoke here | **Aqui tem muita fumaça** |
| | *ahkee tehn moo-eentah foomahsah* |

| It's faulty, can you change it? | **É defeituoso, posso trocar?** |
| | *eh dehfeh-eetoh-oosoo, pohsoo trookar?* |

| The coffee is cold | **O café está frio** |
| | *oo kafeh shtah free-oo* |

| The bill is wrong | **A conta está errada** |
| | *ah kohntah shtah ehrahdah* |

| The dress / suit has a hole in it | **A roupa tem um buraco** |
| | *ah roh-oopah tehn oon boorahkoo* |

| The tablecloth is not clean | **A toalha não é limpa** |
| | *ah too-ahlyah naoon eh leempah* |

| This meat is tough | **Esta carne é dura** |
| | *eshtah karneh eh doorah* |

| This doesn't work | **Isto não funciona** |
| | *eeshtoo naoon foonsyohnah* |

| We are still waiting to be served | **Ainda estamos à espera de ser servidos** |
| | *ah-eendah shtahmoosh ah shpehrah deh ser serveedoosh* |

| I think you have given me the wrong change | **Acho que se enganou no troco** |
| | *ahshoo keh seh eengahnoh-oo noo trohkoo* |

What's your name?	**Qual é o seu nome?** *kwahl eh oo seh-oo nohmeh?*
My name is …	**Eu chamo-me(P)… Me chamo(B)…** *eh-oo shahmoo-meh (P) … mee shahmoo (B) …*
I'm American / British	**Sou americano(a) / britânico(a)** *soh ahmayreekahnu(ah) / breetahneekoh(ah)*
Do you mind if I sit here?	**Posso sentar aqui?** *pohsoo sehntar ahkee?*
I don't speak Portuguese (well)	**Eu não falo (bem) português** *eh-oo naoon fahloo (behn) portoogesh*
Do you speak English?	**Fala inglês?** *fahlah eenglesh?*
Excuse me / Sorry	**Com licença / Desculpe** *kohn leezehnsah / deshkoolpeh*
May I get you a coffee?	**Posso oferecer-lhe(P) lhe oferecer(B) um café?** *pohsoo ohfehrehzer-lyeh (P) lyee ohfehrehzer (B) oon kafeh?*
Not at all / Don't mention it	**Por favor / De nada** *poor favor / deh nahdah*
Yes, please	**Sim, por favor** *seen, poor favor*
No, thank you (very much)	**Não, (muito) obrigado** *naoon, (moo-eentoo) obreegahdoo*
I am here on holiday / on business	**Estou aqui de férias / a trabalho** *shtoh-oo ahkee deh feree-ash / ah trahbahlyoo*

Monday	**segunda-feira**	*sehgoondah-feh-eerah*
Tuesday	**terça-feira**	*tersah-feh-eerah*
Wednesday	**quarta-feira**	*kwartah-feh-eerah*
Thursday	**quinta-feira**	*keentah-feh-eerah*
Friday	**sexta-feira**	*seshtah-feh-eerah*
Saturday	**sábado**	*sahbahdoo*
Sunday	**domingo**	*doomeengoo*

January	**janeiro**	*jahneh-eeroo*
February	**fevereiro**	*fehvehreh-eeroo*
March	**março**	*marsoo*
April	**abril**	*ahbreel*
May	**maio**	*mah-eeoo*
June	**junho**	*joonyoo*
July	**julho**	*joolyoo*
August	**agosto**	*ahgoshtoo*
September	**setembro**	*sehtehmbroo*
October	**outubro**	*oh-ootoobroo*
November	**novembro**	*nohvehmbroo*
December	**dezembro**	*dehzehmbroo*

| Last year | **o ano passado** |
| | *oo ahnoo pahsahdoo* |

| Next week | **a semana que vem** |
| | *ah sehmahnah keh vehn* |

| In / for two days | **daqui a / desde há dois dias** |
| | *dakee ah / deshdeh ah doh-eesh deeash* |

| 1997 | **mil novecentos e noventa e sete** |
| | *meel nohvehsehntoosh ee noovehnta ee seh-teh* |

What road / street is this?	**Que rua/avenida é esta?** *keh roo-ah / ahvehneedah eh eshtah?*
How do we get to the airport?	**Como é que se faz para chegar ao aeroporto?** *kohmoo eh keh seh fash parah shegar ah-oo ah-erohportoo?*
Where can I find a taxi?	**Aonde é que posso tomar (P) pegar (B) um táxi?** *ah-ohndeh eh keh pohsoo toomar (P) pehgar (B) oon tahksee?*
Is this the way to...	**É esta a rua que vai para...** *eh eshtah ah roo-ah keh vah-ee parah ...*
Can you tell me the way to get to ...?	**Qual é a rua para chegar ao / à...** *kwahl eh ah roo-ah parah shegar ah-oo/ ah ...*
How long does it take to get there?	**Quanto tempo se demora para chegar?** *kwahntoo tehmpoo seh dehmorah parah shegar?*
Excuse me, where is the subway station?	**Por favor, aonde é o metro(P) metrô(B)?** *por favor, ah-ohndeh eh oo metroo(P) metroh(B)?*
Excuse me, where is the bus stop?	**Por favor, aonde é a paragen do autocarro(P), aonde é que se pega o ônibus(B)?** *por favor, ah-ohndeh eh ah pahrahdjehn doo ah-ootokaroo (P), ah-ohndeh eh keh see pehgah ohneeboosh(B)?*

Excuse me, can you tell me where the... Restaurant is?	**Desculpe, sabe aonde é o restaurante...?** *deshkoolpeh, sahbeh ah-ohndeh eh oo restah-oorahnteh...?*
Could you show me on the map?	**Pode-me mostrar no mapa?** *pohdeh-meh moostrar noo mahpah?*
Does this bus / train go to ...?	**Este autocarro/comboio vai para...?** *eshteh ah-ootohkahroo/kohmbohyoo vah-ee parah...?*
Which bus / train must I get for ...?	**Qual é o número do autocarro que vai para...?** *kwahl eh oo noomeroo doo ah-ootokahroo keh vah-ee parah...*
Where must I change / get off?	**Onde é que mudo/desço?** *ohndeh eh keh moodo / deshoo?*
I am looking for the tourist information office	**Procuro o turismo** *prohkooroo oo tooreesmoo*

YOU MAY BE TOLD: _____

Não sei
naoon seh-ee

I don't know

**Tem que tomar o autocarro(P)
pegar o ônibus(B)... até...**
*tehn keh toomar oo ah-ootohkaroo (P)
pehgar oo ohneeboosh (B) ... ahteh ...*

You must get bus
number ...
as far as ...

Vá em frente / à direita / à esquerda
*vah ehn frehnteh / ah deereh-eetah /
ah skerdah*

Go straight
ahead/to the right /
to the left

Vire na segunda rua
veereh nah sehgoondah roo-ah

Take the second
street

Do you have you any foreign beers? Which ones?

Vocês têm cervejas importadas? Quais?
vohsesh teh-eem serveh-eejash eemportahdash? kwah-eesh?

A coffee, please

Um café, por favor
oon kahfeh, poor favor

Two cups of tea with lemon

Dois chás com limão
doh-eesh shash kohn leemaoon

That's enough, thank you

Chega, obrigado
shehgah, ohbreegahdoo

What is this / that?

O que é isto/aquilo?
oo keh eh eeshtoo /ahkeeloo?

The bill (separate bills /all together)

A conta (contas separadas / tudo junto)
ah kohntah (kohntash sehpahrahdash / toodoo joontoo)

You haven't brought…

Não trouxe…
naoon troh-ooseh…

I didn't order this, I asked for…

Não pedi isto, pedi…
naoon pehdee eeshtoo, pehdee…

Would you give me a glass of water, please?

Um copo de água, por favor
oon kohpoo deh ahgwah, poor favor

With ice, please

Com gelo, por favor
kohn jehloo, poor favor

I would like an orange juice

Um sumo(P) suco(B) de laranja
oon soomoo (P) sookoh (B) deh lahrahnjah

A gin and tonic, please	**Um gin tônica, por favor** *oon djeen tohneekah, poor favor*
A white martini with an olive	**Um martini branco com uma azeitona** *oon marteenee brankoo kohn oomah* *ahzeh-eetohnah*
A bottle of sparkling water	**Uma garrafa de água com gás** *oomah garahfah deh ahgwah kohn gash*
I'd like an aperitif	**Queria um aperitivo** *kehreeah oon ahpereeteevoo*

YOU MIGHT BE TOLD:

Acabou *ahkaboh-oo*	There is no more
Não temos *naoon tehmoosh*	We don't have any
Pague na caixa *pahgeh nah kah-eeshah*	Pay at the cash-desk

Is there a cheap restaurant near here?	**Tem um restaurante barato aqui perto?** *tehn oon resh_tah-oorahntesh bahrahtoo ahkee pertoo?*
How do I get to the... Restaurant?	**Como é que se chega ao restaurante...?** *kohmoo eh keh seh shehgah ah-oo reshtah-oorahnteh...?*
Where is there a restaurant with typical food?	**Onde é um restaurante de cozinha típica?** *ohndeh eh oon reshtah-oorahnteh deh koozeenyah teepeekah?*
Which is the best restaurant in town?	**Qual é o melhor restaurante da cidade?** *kwahl eh oo mehlyor reshtah-oorahnteh dah seedahdeh?*
How much does it cost per person?	**Quanto se paga por pessoa?** *kwahntoo seh pahgah por pehssoh-ah?*
I'd like a meal in an international/ Chinese restaurant	**Queria almoçar em um restaurante de cozinha internacional/chinesa** *kehree-ah ahlmoosar eh oon reshtah-oorahnteh deh koozeenyah eenternahsyohnahl/sheenehzah*
We would like to have supper in a restaurant that is not very expensive	**Queríamos jantar em um restaurante não muito caro** *kehree-ahmoosh jahntar ehn oon reshtah-oorahnteh naoon moo-eentoo kahroo*
Are there any good Italian restaurants/ pizza shops?	**Existem bons restaurantes italianos/ pizzarias?** *eeseeeshten bohnsh reshtah-oorahntesh eetahlyahnoosh/peezahree-ash?*

What time does the restaurant open/close?	**A que horas abre/fecha o restaurante?** *ah keh ohrash ahbreh/fehshah oo reshtah-oorahnteh?*
Can I book a table for four?	**É possível reservar uma mesa para quatro?** *eh poosseevehl rehzervar oomah mehzah pahrah kwahtroo?*
I'd like to cancel a booking I made for this evening in the name of…	**Queria desmarcar uma reserva que fiz para hoje à noite, em nome de…** *kehree-ah deshmarkar oomah rezervah keh feesh pahrah ohjeh ah noh-eeteh ehn nohmeh deh…*
I'd like to book for lunchtime tomorrow	**Queria reservar para amanhã ao almoço** *kehree-ah rezervar pahrah ahmahnyah ah-oo ahlmohssoo*
I'd like to know if it's necessary to book	**Queria saber se é preciso reservar** *kehree-ah sahber seh eh prehseesoo rezervar*
We have a reservation for nine o'clock	**Temos uma reserva para as nove horas** *tehmoosh oomah rezervah pahrah ash nohveh ohrash*
Have you a fixed-price/tourist menu?	**Vocês têm um menu fixo / turístico?** *vohssesh teh-eem oon mehnoo feeksoo/ tooreesteekoo*
Is there an entrance for the disabled?	**Existe uma entrada para deficientes?** *eeseeshteh oomah ehntrahdah pahrah dehfeesyehntesh?*

Do you speak English?	**Fala inglês?** *fahlah eenglesh?*
I'd like a table in a quieter place	**Queria uma mesa num lugar mais calmo** *kehree-ah oomah mehrah noon loogar maeesh kalmoo*
We'd like a table for two/outside	**Queremos uma mesa para dois/ ao ar livre** *kehreemoosh oomah mehzah pahrah doh-eesh/ah-oo ahr leevreh*
Waiter!	**Garçon!** *garsohn!*
May we see the menu?	**Podemos ver o menu?** *poodehmoosh ver oo mehnoo?*
Do you have a vegetarian menu?	**Tem um menu vegetariano?** *tehn oon mehnoo vehdjehtahree-ahnoo?*
What do you suggest?	**Qual é a sua sugestão?** *kwahl eh ah soo-ah soojeshtaoon?*
What is the restaurant's specialty?	**Como é a especialidade da casa?** *kohmoo eh ah shpehsee-ahleedahdeh dah kahzah?*
What is today's choice?	**Qual é o prato do dia?** *kwahl eh oo prahtoo doo dee-ah?*
What dishes are typical of this area?	**Quais são os pratos típicos da região?** *kwah-eesh saoon oos prahtoosh teepeekoosh dah rehdjaoon?*

What are the ingredients of this dish?	**De que coisa é feito este prato?** *deh keh koh-eezah eh feh-eetoo eshteh prahtoo?*
Is it (very) hot/sweet?	**É (muito) picante/doce?** *eh (moo-eento) peekahnteh/dohsseh?*
I'd like a half-portion of…	**Queria meia porção de…** *kehree-ah meh-eeyah porsaoon deh…*
Can you change the fork/ knife/spoon?	**Pode-me trocar o garfo/a faca/ a colher?** *pohdeh-meh trookar oo gargoo/ ah fahkah/ah koolyer?*
Can you bring me another glass/ napkin?	**Pode-me trazer outro copo/ guardanapo?** *pohdeh-meh trahzer oh-ootroo kohpoo/ gwardahnahpoo?*
Could you bring me a coffee?	**Pode-me trazer um café?** *pohdeh-meh trahzer oon kahfeh?*
What sweets/fruit do you have?	**Que doces/frutas vocês têm?** *keh dohssesh/frootash vohssesh teh-eem?*
Does this dish contain garlic/ pepper?	**Este prato tem alho/pimenta?** *eshteh prahtoo tehn ahlyoo/peemehntah?*
Can it be done without onion/salt?	**Pode-se fazer sem cebola/sal?** *pohdeh-see fahzer sehn sehbohlah/sahl?*
Rare/medium/ well done, please	**Mal passado/médio/bem passado, por favor** *mahl pahssahdoo/mehdyoo/behn pahssahdoo, por favor*

What wine do you suggest with this dish?

Que vinho nos aconselha com este prato?
keh veenyoo noosh ahkohnsehlyah kohn eshteh prahtoo?

Bring us your house wine

Traga o vinho da casa
trahgah oo veenyoo dah kahzah

Bring us another jug / can of ...

Outra jarro/lata de...
oh-ootroo jahroo / lahtah deh ...

Can you suggest a good white / red wine for us?

Pode sugerir um bom vinho branco/tinto?
pohdeh soojehreer oon bohn veenyoo brahnkoo / teentoo?

Can you bring me some ice / lemon?

Pode trazer gelo/limão?
pohdeh trahzer djehloo / leemaoon?

May I have the wine list?

Posso ver a carta dos vinhos?
pohsoo ver ah kartah doosh veenyoosh?

Can you put the bottle to chill?

Pode pôr a garrafa no gelo?
pohdeh por ah gahrahfah noo djehloo?

Which spirits/whisky do you have?

Quais são os licores/whiskies que vocês têm?
kwaeesh saoon oos leekohresh / whiskies keh vosesh teh-een?

What are the wines/spirits of this region?

Quais são os vinhos/licores da região?
kwaeesh saoon oos veenyoosh/leekohresh dah rehdjaoon?

A bottle of fizzy water

Uma garrafa de água com gás
oomah gahrahfah deh ahgwah kohn gash

Where is the toilet?	**Onde é a toilette?** *ohndeh eh ah too-ahlehteh?*
May I have an ashtray?	**Pode trazer um cinzeiro?** *pohdeh trahzer oon seenseh-eeroo?*
May I use the telephone, please?	**Posso usar o telefone, por favor?** *pohsoo oozar oo tehlehfohneh, por favor?*
Can you call a taxi, please?	**Pode chamar um taxi, por favor?** *pohdeh shahmar oon tahksee, por favor?*
Can you turn the music down?	**Poderia abaixar a música?** *poodehree-ah ahbah-eeshar ah moozeekah?*
Can you turn up the heating/the air conditioning?	**Pode aumentar o aquecimento/ o ar condicionado?** *pohdeh ah-oomehntar oo akehseemehntoo/ oo ar kohndeesyohnahdoo?*
Can you open/shut the window?	**Pode abrir/fechar a janela?** *pohdeh ahbreer/feshar ah jahnehlah?*

Is there anyone here who speaks English?
Tem alguém que fale inglês?
tehn algehn keh faleh eenglesh?

Is there a doctor here?
Tem um médico aqui?
tehn oon mehdeekoo ahkee?

Call a doctor / an ambulance!
Alguém chame um médico/ uma ambulância!
ahlgen shahmeh oon mehdeekoo/ oomah ahmboolahnsee-ah!

Where is the nearest hospital?
Onde é o hospital mais perto daqui?
ohndeh eh oo oshpeetahl mah-eesh pertoo dakee?

I must go to the police
Tenho que ir à polícia
tehnyoo keh eer ah pooleesee-ah

Where is a pharmacy?
Aonde é a farmácia?
ah-ohndeh eh ah farmahsee-ah?

I must go to the dentist
Tenho que ir ao dentista
tehnyoo keh eer aoo dehnteestah

I have had an accident
Tive um acidente
teeveh oon ahzeedehnteh

I need an interpreter/ a lawyer
Preciso de um intérprete/advogado
prehzeezoo deh oon eenterprehteh / ahdvoogahdoo

I have lost my bag / my son
Perdi a minha bolsa/o meu filho
perdee ah meenyah bohlsah / meh-oo feelyoo

I have lost my credit card
Perdi o meu cartão de crédito
perdee ah meh-oo kartaoon deh krehdeetoo

I don't feel well	**Não me sinto bem** *naoon meh seentoo behn*
Can you help me?	**Pode ajudar-me(P)? Pode me ajudar(B)?** *pohdeh ahjoodar-meh (P)? pohdjee mee ajoodar (B)?*
Somebody help me, please	**Alguém me ajude, por favor** *ahlgehn meh ahjoodeh, poor favor*
I've run out of gas	**Fiquei sem gasolina** *feekeh-ee sehn gahsooleenah*
I've been robbed / injured	**Fui roubado(a)/ferido(a)** *foo-ee roh-oobahdoo(ah) / fehreedoo(ah)*
Fire!	**Há fogo!** *ah fohgoo!*

Is there any show suitable for children?

Existe algum espetáculo para as crianças?
eezeeshteh ahlgoom eeshpetahkooloo pahrah ash kree-ahnsash?

Are there any interesting shows / plays?

Existem espetáculos/teatros interessantes?
eezeeshtehn eeshpetahkooloosh / tee-ahtroosh eentehrehsahntesh?

Are there any discotheques/ piano-bars?

Existem discotecas/piano-bar?
eezeeshtehn deescootehkash / pee-ahnoo-bar?

Are there any excursions we make?

Existem excursões para fazer?
eezeeshtehn shkoorsoh-eensh pahrah fahzer?

Can we reserve two seats?

Podemos reservar dois lugares?
poodehmoosh rehzervar doh-eesh loogaresh?

Can you reserve the tickets for us?

É possível reservar os bilhetes(P) ingressos(B)?
eh pooseevel rehzervar oos beelee-ehtesh (P) eengrehsoosh (B)?

What is the entrance fee?

Quanto custa o bilhete(P) ingresso(B)?
kwahntoo kooshtah oo beelee-ehteh (P) eengrehsoo (B)?

Can we rent ...?

Pode-se(P) Se pode(B) alugar...?
pohdeh-seh (P) see pohdjee (B) aloogar ...?

Can we go riding / fishing?

Pode-se(P) Se pode(B) andar a cavalo/ pescar?
pohdeh-seh (P) see pohdjee (B) ahndar ah kahvahloo / peshkar?

Good evening/night	**Boa noite** *boh-ah noh-eeteh*
Good morning	**Bom dia** *bohn dee-ah*
Good afternoon	**Boa tarde** *boh-ah tardeh*
How are you? (formal)	**Como está?** *kohmoo shtah?*
How are you? (informal)	**Como é que estás(P)? Tudo bem(B)?** *kohmoo eh keh shtash(P)? toodoo behn(B)?*
How do you do? Pleased to meet you	**Muito prazer/É um prazer** *moo-eentoo prahzer/eh oon prahzer*
Hi! Hullo!	**Olá(P)! Oi(B)!** *ohlah(P)! oh-ee(B)!*
See you later	**Até logo** *ahteh lohgoo*
Bye-bye! See you!	**Tchau!** *chah-oo!*
Goodbye	**Adeus** *ahdeh-oosh*
(All) right/well, thank you	**(Tudo) Bem, obrigado** *(toodoo) behn, ohbreegahdoo*

What are these / those?	**O que são estas / estes...** *oo keh saoon eshtash / eshtesh ...*
What is it made of?	**É feito de quê?** *eh feh-eetoo deh keh?*
Is this cheese fresh?	**É fresco este queijo?** *eh freskoo eshteh keh-eejoo?*
I would like two bottles	**Queria duas garrafas** *kereeah dooash gahrahfash*
How long does it keep?	**Por quanto tempo se conserva?** *por kwantoo tempoo seh kohnservah?*
I prefer that / this	**Prefiro aquele(a)/este(a)** *prehfeeroo akehleh(ah) /eshteh(a)*
Can you wrap it for me for the trip?	**Pode embrulhar-me para viagem?** *pohdeh ehmbroolyar-meh pahra veeahdjen?*
How much is it a kilo?	**Quanto custa ao kilo/quilo?** *kwantoo kooshtah aoo keeloo?*
I'd like a chocolate ice cream	**Queria um sorvete de chocolate** *kereeah oon sorvehteh deh shookohlahteh*

ARTICLES

The articles in Portuguese indicate the gender and number of the noun:

Definite Articles: The

o	m. sing.	**o castelo**	the castle
a	f. sing.	**a mesa**	the table
os	m. pl.	**os animais**	the animals
as	f. pl	**as cadeiras**	the chairs

Indefinite Articles: A/An

um	m. sing.	**um castelo**	a castle
uma	f. sing.	**uma mesa**	a table
uns	m. pl.	**uns animais**	animals
umas	f. pl.	**umas cadeiras**	chairs

N.B.: Some articles are articulated with prepositions in one word; for example:

to the	**a**	f. sing.	**ao**	m. sing.
of the	**da**	f. sing.	**do**	m. sing.
in the	**na**	f. sing.	**no**	m. sing.
to the	**as**	f. pl.	**aos**	m. pl.
of the	**das**	f. pl.	**dos**	m. pl
in the	**nas**	f. pl.	**nos**	m. pl.

MASCULINE AND FEMININE NOUNS

You can generally tell if a word is masculine or feminine by its ending:
– the **-o**, **-or,** and **-l endings** indicate masculine nouns which require the masculine articles:

o natal	(the) Christmas	**o hotel**	the hotel
o carro	the car	**o cheiro**	the smell

– the **-a**, **-e**, **-agem**, and **-dade** endings indicate feminine nouns requiring feminine articles:

a casa	the house	**a coragem**	the courage
a idade	the age	**a felicidade**	the happiness

Here are some exceptions and words with different endings:

o homem/a mulher	the man / the woman
o irmão/a irmã	the brother / the sister
o pai/a mãe	the father / the mother

PLURALS

As a general rule, the words ending in a vowel form the plural by adding **-s**; those ending in a consonant take **-es**:

cama/camas	bed / beds
mulher/mulheres	woman / women
tapete/tapetes	carpet / carpets
mês/meses	month / months

The following are exceptions:

a final -m becomes **-ns in the plural**
homem/homens man /men

-l in the plural becomes **-is**
carnaval/carnavais carnival / carnivals

-s is invariable:
pires/pires saucer / saucers

-ão, the most common plurals of which are:
-ões atenção/atenções attention / attentions
-ãos mão/mãos hand / hands

DIMINUTIVES AND AUGMENTATIVES

– Words ending in an unstressed vowel form the diminutives
with **-inho/-inha**:
menino/menininho   boy / little boy

– Words ending in a consonant or a stressed vowel form the
diminutive by taking **-zinho/-zinha**:
café/cafezinho   coffee / small coffee

The augmentatives (= "big"), which are almost always used
with a negative meaning, are usually formed with the **-ão** for
the masculine and the **-ona** for the feminine.

ADJECTIVES

Adjectives normally follow the nouns, and agree in gender and
number; for the plurals, the rules are the same as for nouns:

– they are invariable (that is, they are the same for the
masculine and for the feminine) when they end in **-e**, **-al**, **-el**,
-il, **-az**, **-iz**, **-oz**:
um homem feliz / uma mulher feliz
a happy man / a happy woman

o ingrediente natural / a erva natural
the natural ingredient / the natural grass

– adjectives which end in **-o** in the masculine become **-a in
the feminine**:
um lugar bonito / uma cidade bonita
a beautiful place / a beautiful city

– adjectives which end in **-ão** become **-ã in the feminine**:
alemão/alemã   German (m.) / German (f.)

– the following adjectives have irregular feminine forms:
bom/boa   good
mau/má   bad

DEMONSTRATIVE ADJECTIVES AND PRONOUNS

There are three demonstrative adjectives and pronouns
which form the plural (with the final **-s**) and the feminine
(with the final **-a**) regularly:

este libro   this book
esse copo   this glass
aquele avião   that plane

There are also some neutral forms which are invariable and
have neither plural nor feminine forms:

isto this   **isso** this, that   **aquilo** that

POSSESSIVE ADJECTIVES AND PRONOUNS

Masc.	Fem.	
meu	**minha**	my; mine
teu	**tua**	your; yours
seu	**sua**	his; his / her; hers /its
nosso	**nossa**	our; ours
vosso	**vossa**	your; yours
seu	**sua**	their; theirs

The plural is formed according to the rule, adding the final **-s**.

Seeing that the forms of the third person, **seu** and **sua**, are identical in the singular and in the plural, in Portuguese the words **dele**, **dela**, **deles** and **delas** (respectively, belonging to him, to her, to them) are used:

a casa é dele the house is his
os gatos são delas the cats are theirs

PERSONAL PRONOUNS

Singular

I	**eu**	*eh-oo*
me/to me	**me**	*meh*
me	**mim**	*meem*
with me	**comigo**	*koomeegoo*
you	**tu**	*too*
you / to you	**te**	*teh*
you	**ti**	*tee*
with you	**contigo**	*kohnteegoo*
he / she	**ele/ela**	*ehleh/ehlah*
him / her to him /her	**lhe**	*lyee*
him / her	**o/a**	*oo/ah*
himself/ herself	**se**	*seh*
to himself/ herself		
with himself / with herself	**consigo**	*kohnseegoo*
you (formal)	**você**	*vohseh*

Plural

we	**nós**	*nosh*
us / to us	**nos**	*noosh*
with us	**conosco**	*kohnoshkoo*
you	**vós**	*vosh*
you / to you	**vos**	*voosh*
with you	**convosco**	*kohnvoshkoo*
they	**eles/elas**	*ehlesh/ehlash*
them to them	**lhes**	*lyeesh*
them	**os/as**	*oosh/ash*
themselves / to themselves	**se**	*seh*
with themselves	**consigo**	*kohnseegoo*
you (formal)	**vocês**	*vohsesh*

N.B.: In Portugal, personal pronouns are often linked to the verb by a hyphen, while in Brazilian Portuguese pronouns come before the verbs, at least in the spoken language:

Portugal: amo-te; eu disse-lhe
Brazil: te amo; eu lhe disse
(I love you; I told him).

SPEECH FORMS

Informal language

– In Portugal the informal mode of address used in speaking to relatives, close friends, or children is the second person singular of the verb:

és muito gentil   you are very kind

– In Brazil, on the other hand, the pronouns **você** (singular) and **vocês** (plural) are used with verbs in the third person singular or plural when speaking informally:

você é bonita   you are beautiful
vocês são turistas   you are tourists

Formal Language

– The second person plural is no longer used. Both in Portugal and in Brazil, in a formal situation, the form of address most commonly used is the third person (singular or plural) of the verb, preceded by:

o senhor/a senhora	the gentleman / the lady
os senhores/	the gentlemen / the ladies
as senhoras	
A senhora é muito	you are very nice
simpática	
Os senhores são	they are proud
orgulhosos	

INTERROGATIVE PRONOUNS

que? quê?	what?
quem?	who?
qual? quais?	which?
quanto? quanta?	how much?
quantos? quantas?	how many?

RELATIVE PRONOUNS

que	that / which
quem	that / who
o qual/a qual/	which / who(m) (singular)
os quais/as quais	which / who(m) (plural)
cujo/cuja/	whose (singular)
cujos/cujas	whose (plural)

INDEFINITE ADJECTIVES AND PRONOUNS

alguém/algum	some / any (masculine)
uns/alguns	some / any (plural)
algumas/alguma	some / any (feminine)
ninguém	no; nobody
nenhum/nenhuma	no; none
nada	nothing

VERBS

N.B.: As already explained in "Speech Forms," the second person plural is no longer used and is therefore omitted in the following conjugations.

The verb endings are: **-ar**, **-er**, **-ir** in the infinitive. Regular verbs are conjugated keeping the root form and changing the endings, as in the examples below.

falar (to speak)	**com**er (to eat)	**part**ir (to leave)
Present		
eu (I) **falo**	como	parto
tu (you) **falas**	comes	partes
ele/ela (he/she) **fala**	come	parte
nós (we) **falamos**	comemos	partimos
eles/elas (they) **falam**	comem	partem
Simple Past		
falei	comi	parti
falaste	comeste	partiste
falou	comeu	partiu
falamos	comemos	partimos
falaram	comeram	partiram
Future		
falarei	comerei	partirei
falarás	comerás	partirás
falará	comerá	partirá
falaremos	comeremos	partiremos
falarão	comerão	partirão

AUXILIARY VERBS

ser (to be)	estar (to be)	ter (to have)

Present

eu (I) sou	estou	tenho
tu (you) és	estás	tens
ele/ela (he/she) é	está	tem
nós (we) somos	estamos	temos
eles/elas (they) são	estão	têm

Simple Past

fui	estive	tive
foste	estiveste	tiveste
foi	esteve	teve
fomos	estivemos	tivemos
foram	estiveram	tiveram

Future

serei	estarei	terei
serás	estarás	terás
será	estará	terá
seremos	estaremos	teremos
serão	estarão	terão

The present indicative of some of the most common irregular verbs:

ir (to go)	fazer (to do, to make)	saber (to know)	ver (to see)	vir (to come)
vou	faço	sei	vejo	venho
vais	fazes	sabes	vês	vens
vai	faz	sabe	vê	vem
vamos	fazemos	sabemos	vemos	vimos
vão	fazem	sabem	vêem	vêm

New Year's Day	**Fim de Ano (P) Revéillon (B)**
Carnival	**Carnaval**
Ash Wednesday	**Dia de Finados**
Palm Sunday	**Domingo de Ramos**
Epiphany	**Dia dos Reis Magos** (6 January)
Labor Day	**Dia do Trabalho** (1 May)
Immaculate Conception	**Dia da Imaculada Conceição** (8 December)
Liberation Day	**25 de Abril (P)** (25 April) **Independência (B)** (7 September)
Christmas	**Natal**
All Saints	**Dia de Todos os Santos** (1 November)
Easter	**Páscoa**
Holy Week	**Semana Santa**

We will arrive on the …	**Chegamos no dia…** *shegahmoosh noo dee-ah ….*
We will stay for 3 nights, from the … to the …	**Vamos ficar por três noites, do dia… até ao…** *vahmoosh feekahr poor tresh noh-eetesh, doo dee-ah … ahteh aoo …*
Is breakfast included in the price?	**O pequeno-almoço(P) café da manhã(B) é incluído no preço?** *oo pehkehnoo-ahlmohssoo (P) kahfeh dah manyah (B) eh eenkloo-eedoo noo pressoo?*
How much is it per day / per week?	**Quanto custa ao dia / à semana?** *kwahntoo kooshtah aoo dee-ah / ah sehmahnah?*
I'd like to book a single / double room	**Queria reservar uma suíte single/ de casal** *kehree-ah rehzervahr ooma sweeteh single / deh kasahl*

YOU MAY BE TOLD: ─────────────

É um serviço à parte
eh oon serveehsoo ah pahrteh

This service is charged separately

Estamos cheios
shtahmoosh sheh-eeoosh

We are fully booked

Não temos vagas nesse período
naoon tehmoosh vahgash nehsseh peree-oodoo

We have nothing available for that period

What time is breakfast / lunch / supper?	**A que horas é o pequeno-almoço(P) café-da-manhã(B) / almoço / jantar?** *ah keh orash eh oo pehkehnoo ahlmohssoo (P) kahfeh dah manyah (B)/ ahlmohssoo / jahntahr?*
We booked a room in the name of	**Fizemos uma reserva em nome de…** *feezehmoosh oomah rezehrvah ehn nohmeh deh ….*
Do you have a babysitting service?	**Vocês têm um serviço de baby-sitter?** *vohssesh teh-eem oon serveessoo deh baby-sitter?*
Is there a phone/ TV / bathroom in the room?	**Tem telefone / televisão / casa de banho(P) banheiro(B) no quarto?** *tehn telefohneh / tehlehveesaoon / kahzah deh banyoo (P) banye-eeroo (B) noo kwartoo?*
Is there heating/ air conditioning in the room?	**Tem aquecimento/ar condicionado no quarto?** *tehn akezeemehntoo / ahr kondeesyoonahdoo noo kwartoo?*
Put it on my bill	**Meta na minha conta** *mehtah nah meenyah kohntah*
We would like to have breakfast in our room at	**Queríamos o pequeno-almoço(P) café-da-manhã(B) no quarto às…** *kereeyahmoosh oo pekehnoo almohssoo (P) kahfeh dah manyah (B) noo kwartoo ash …*
May I have my key?	**A minha chave, por favor** *ah meenyah shahveh, poor favor?*
Can you wake us at 8 o'clock?	**Pode-nos acordar às oito horas?** *pohdeh-noosh akordar ash oh-eetoo ohrash?*

I don't have
enough money

Não tenho dinheiro suficiente
*naoon tehnyoo deenyeh-eeroo
soofeezyehnteh*

Can you change a
... note?

**Pode-me(P) Me pode(B) trocar uma
nota de...?**
*pohdeh-meh (P) mee pohdjee (B)
trookar oomah nohtah deh...?*

What is the
exchange
rate for the dollar /
for the pound?

**Qual é o câmbio do dólar / dah
esterlina?**
*kwahl eh oo kahmbyoo doo dohlar /
dah ehshtehrleenah ?*

I have no
money left

Fiquei sem dinheiro
feekeh-ee sehn deenyeh-eeroo

I would like to
change dollars /
pounds into
escudos / reals

**Queria trocar dólares/ em escudos/
reais**
*kehree-ah trookar dohlaresh / ehn
shkoodosh / reh-ah-eesh*

I would like to sell/
buy / change /
deposit

**Queria vender/comprar/trocar/
depositar**
*kehree-ah vehnder / kohmprar /trookar /
dehpoozeetar*

0 zero	**15 quinze**	**90 noventa**
zeroo	*keenzeh*	*novehntah*
1 um	**16 dezasseis**	**100 cem**
oon	*dehzaseh-eesh*	*sehn*
2 dois	**17 dezassete**	**101 cento e um**
doh-eesh	*dehzasehteh*	*sehntoo ee oon*
3 três	**18 dezoito**	**110 cento e dez**
tresh	*dehzoh-eetoo*	*sehntoo ee desh*
4 quatro	**19 dezanove**	**200 duzentos**
kwahtroo	*dehzahnohveh*	*doozehntoosh*
5 cinco	**20 vinte**	**300 trezentos**
seenkoo	*veenteh*	*trezehntoosh*
6 seis	**21 vinte e um**	**400 quatrocentos**
seh-eesh	*veenteh ee oon*	*kwahtroozehntoosh*
7 sete	**22 vinte e dois**	**500 quinhentos**
sehteh	*veenteh ee doh-eesh*	*keenyehntoosh*
8 oito	**23 vinte e três**	**600 seiscentos**
oh-eetoo	*veenteh ee tresh*	*seh-eeshsehntoosh*
9 nove	**30 trinta**	**700 setecentos**
nohveh	*treentah*	*sehtehsehntoosh*
10 dez	**40 quarenta**	**800 oitocentos**
desh	*kwahrehntah*	*oh-eetoosehntoosh*
11 onze	**50 cinquenta**	**900 novecentos**
ohnzeh	*seenkwehntah*	*nohvehsehntoosh*
12 doze	**60 sessenta**	**1000 mil**
dohzeh	*sehsehntah*	*meel*
13 treze	**70 setenta**	**5000 cinco mil**
trehze	*sehtehntah*	*seenkoo meel*
14 quatorze	**80 oitenta**	**1000000 um milhão**
kahtorze	*oh-eetehntah*	*oon meelyaoon*

1st primeiro	**4th quarto**	**7th sétimo**	**10th décimo**
preemeh-eeroo	*kwartoo*	*sehteemoo*	*dehseemoo*
2nd segundo	**5th quinto**	**8th oitavo**	
sehgoondoo	*keentoo*	*oh-eetahvoo*	
3rd terceiro	**6th sexto**	**9th nono**	
terseh-eeroo	*seh-eeshtoo*	*nohnoo*	

PAYING

How much does it cost?	**Quanto custa?** *kwahntoo kooshtah?*
How much is that in all?	**Quanto é tudo?** *kwahntoo eh toodoo?*
Must I pay in advance?	**Tenho que pagar adiantado?** *tehnyoo keh pahgar ahdyahntahdoo?*
Is that with the discount?	**É já com desconto?** *eh jah kohn deshkohntoo?*
Can't you give me a discount?	**Não pode fazer um desconto?** *naoon pohdeh fahzer oon deshkohntoo?*
Is service / tax included?	**O serviço/imposto é incluído?** *oo serveesoo / eemposhtoo eh eenkloo-eedoo?*
Will you bring the bill, please?	**Pode-me trazer a conta, por favor?** *pohdeh-meh trahzer ah kohntah, por favor?*
May I see the price list?	**Posso ver a lista de preços?** *pohsoo ver ah leeshtah deh presoosh?*
May I pay by credit card?	**Posso pagar com cartão de crédito?** *pohsoo pahgar kohn kartaoon deh krehdeetoo?*
Do you accept checks/travelers' checks?	**Vocês aceitam cheques / travelers' checks?** *vosesh ahseh-eetahn shehkesh / trahvehlehrs shehkesh*
I'd like the receipt	**Queria um recibo(P) uma nota fiscal(B)** *kehree-ah oon reseeboo (P) oomah nohtah feeshkah-oo(B)*

I need help	**Preciso de ajuda** *prehseezoo deh ahjoodah*
I need an interpreter	**Preciso de um intérprete** *prehseezoo deh oon eenterprehteh*
Leave me alone!	**Deixe-me(P) Me deixe(B) em paz!** *deh-eesheh-meh (P) mee deh-eeshee (B)* *ehn pash!*
I am lost	**Perdi-me(P) Me perdi(B)** *perdee-meh (P) mee perdjee (B)*
I don't understand	**Não percebo(P) entendo(B)** *naoon persehboo (P) eentehndoo (B)*
Do you speak English?	**Fala inglês?** *fahlah eenglesh?*
Can you help me, please?	**Pode-me(P) Me pode(B) ajudar?** *pohdeh-meh (P) mee pohdjee ahjoodar?*
Can you speak more slowly?	**Pode falar mais devagar?** *pohdeh fahlah mah-eesh dehvahgar?*
Can you say that again, please?	**Pode repetir, por favor?** *pohdeh rehpehteer, por favor?*
What's the problem?	**Qual é o problema?** *kwahl eh oo prooblehmah?*
I think there is a mistake in the bill	**Acho que tem um erro nesta conta** *ashoo keh tehn oon eroo neshtah* *kohntah*

In order to make the pronunciation of the phrases in this book easy and accurate, we here give you symbols to represent as closely as possible the Portuguese sounds. The stressed sound or syllable in each word is underlined. Slight differences, especially in vowel sounds, are difficult to reproduce visually without using sophisticated phonetics, therefore this guide has intentionally used a simplified system.

As in all living languages, Portuguese contains many exceptions to the rules. For this reason there will be cases in which the italicized pronunciation indicated under the Portuguese sentences differs from the general rules given below. Further differences may occur between Portuguese and Brazilian; for example the word for mustard, **mostarda**, is pronounced *moshtardah* in Brazil and *mooshtardah* in Portugal.

The letters not listed here should be pronounced in approximately the same way as in Standard English.

Vowels & Symbol diphthongs:		Portuguese word	
á, à, ó	*ah, oh*	**casa, pò**	*kahzah, poh*
â, ô	*ah, oh*	**pâra, dor**	*pahrah, dohr*
é, è, ê	*eh*	**café**	*kahfeh*
i	*ee* as in seen	**frio**	*free-oo*
o	*oo* at the end of a word, sometimes in the middle in Portuguese	**carro**	*kahroo*
u	*oo* as in noon	**uvas**	*oovash*
ão	*aoon*	**pão**	*paoon*
ãe	*aee*	**mãe**	*maeen*
ões	*oeensh*	**melões**	*mehloeensh*

Consonants:

ce, ci	*seh* as in <u>send</u> *see* as in see	cinema	*seen<u>eh</u>mah*
ç	*s*	peça	*peh<u>s</u>ah*
ch	*sh*	chave	*<u>sh</u>ahveh*
di	*dee* (in Portugal) *djee* (in Brazil)	dia	*<u>dee</u>-ah* *<u>djee</u>-ah*
ge, gi	*dj* as in <u>g</u>em, <u>g</u>in	girar	*<u>dj</u>ee<u>r</u>ar*
gue, gui	*g* as in <u>g</u>et, <u>g</u>ive	guerra	*<u>g</u>ehrah*
j	*j* as in pleasure	janela	*<u>j</u>ahnehlah*
lh	*ly* as in mi<u>lli</u>on	alho	*ah<u>ly</u>oo*
nh	*ny* as in o<u>ni</u>on	banho	*bah<u>ny</u>oo*
que, qui	*keh, kee*	quente	*<u>keh</u>nteh*
s	*sh* (in middle or at end of a word) *z* between vowels	pés desconto casa	*pe<u>sh</u>* *de<u>sh</u>k<u>oh</u>ntoo* *ka<u>h</u>zah*
te	*tchee* (in Brazil)	dente	*d<u>eh</u>ntchee*
x	*sh* (almost always)	peixe	*peh-ee<u>sh</u>eh*
z	(in the middle or at the end) *z*	beleza	*behl<u>eh</u>zah*
z	(final) *sh*	feliz	*fehl<u>eesh</u>*

N.B. When there is also a difference in meaning between the Portuguese and the Brazilian as well as in pronunciation, both forms are presented, the Brazilian form always being marked with the letter **B**.

In our pronunciation guide, we have tried to use the English letters which most closely approximate the Portuguese sounds; follow the symbols given, remembering that each one represents a sound, not a combination of letters.

What is this / that?	**O que é isto / aquilo?** *oo keh eh eeshtoo / ahkeeloo*
What does this mean? What do you mean?	**Qual é o significado? O que quer dizer?** *kwahl eh oo seeg-neefeekahdoo? oo keh ker deezer?*
What did you say?	**Como disse?** *kohmoo deeseh?*
What road /street is this?	**Que rua / avenida é esta?** *keh roo-ah / ahvehneedah eh eshtah?*
Who is this?	**Quem é?** *kehn eh?*
How? Where is it?	**Como? Aonde é?** *kohmoo? ah-ohndeh eh?*
Does it cost a lot / a little?	**Custa muito/pouco?** *kooshtah moo-eentoo / poh-ookoo?*
Where are the shops?	**Aonde são as lojas?** *ah-ohndeh saoon ash lohjash?*
Is it far / near?	**É longe/perto?** *eh lohnjeh / pertoo?*
Do you understand?	**Percebeu(P)? Entendeu(B)?** *persehbeh-oo (P)? eentehndeh-oo (B)?*
Why?	**Porquê?** *poorkeh?*
When? How long?	**Quando? Quanto tempo?** *kwahndoo? kwahntoo tehmpoo?*

Where is the men's/
ladies' room?

**Onde é a toilette dos homens/
das senhoras?**
*ohndeh eh ah too-ahlehteh doosh
ohmensh/dash sehnyorash?*

Is there a toilet
for the disabled?

**Existe uma toilette
para deficientes físicos?**
*eeseeshteh oomah too-ahlehteh pahrah
dehfeesee-ehntesh feezeekoosh?*

Is it a pay toilet?

A toilette é a pagamento?
ah too-ahlehteh eh ah pahgahmehntoo?

The bathroom
is dirty

**A casa de banho(P)
O banheiro(B) é sujo**
*ah kahzah deh bahnyoo(P) oo ahnyeh-
eeroo(B) eh soojoo*

The toilet is blocked/
doesn't work

O water é entupido/não funciona
*oo vahter eh eentoopeedoo/naoon
foonsee-ohnah*

There is no toilet
paper/soap

Não tem papel higiênico/sabonete
*naoon tehn pahpehl eedjehneekoo/
sahboonehteh*

Do you have any matches/lighters?	**Tem fósforos / isqueiro?** *tehn foshfooroosh / eeskeh-eeroo?*
Have you got any pipe tobacco?	**Tem tabaco para cachimbo?** *tehn tahbahkoo parah kasheemboo?*
Where is a tobacconist's?	**Aonde é uma tabacaria?** *ah-ohndeh eh oomah tahbahkaree-ah?*
Do you have any cigars?	**Tem charutos?** *tehn sharootoosh?*
Do you mind if I smoke?	**Incomoda se fumo?** *eenkoomohdah seh foomoo?*
May I have an ashtray?	**Tem um cinzeiro?** *tehn oon seenseh-eeroo?*
Is smoking allowed here?	**Pode-se(P) Se pode(B) fumar aqui?** *pohdeh-seh (P) see pohdjee (B) foomar akee?*
May I offer you a cigarette?	**Aceita um cigarro?** *ahseh-eetah oon seegahroo?*

Can you call a taxi, please?	**Pode-me(P) Me pode(B) chamar um táxi?** *pohdeh-meh(P) mee pohdjee(B) shahmar oon tahksee?*
To the aiport/ to... Road/...Street	**Para o aeroporto/rua/avenida...** *pahrah o ah-erohportoo/ roo-ah/ahvehneedah...*
I have to go to this address	**Tenho que ir nesta morada(P) neste endereço(B)** *tehnyoo keh eer neshtah moorahdah(P) nesh-chee ehndehressoo(B)*
Is it near/far?	**È longe/perto?** *eh lohngeh/pertoo?*
I am in a hurry	**Tenho muita pressa** *tehnyoo moo-eentah pressah*
How much will it cost?	**Quanto custa?** *kwahntoo kooshtah?*
How much do I owe you?	**Quanto é?** *kwahntoo eh?*
Stop here/ at the corner	**Pode parar aqui/ali na esquina** *pohdeh parar ahkee/ahlee nah skeenah*

Hello!	**Pronto/Está lá(P) Alô (B)** *prohntoo/shtah lah(P) ahloh(B)*
Who's speaking?	**Quem fala?** *kehn fahlah?*
I'd like to make a phone call	**Queria fazer uma chamada(P) ligação(B)** *kehree-ah fahzer oomah shahmahdah(P) leegahssaoon(B)*
The number is… extension…	**O número é… extensão…(P) ramal(B)…** *oo noomeroo eh… eshtehnsaoon…(P) rahmah-oo(B)*
I would like a phone card, please	**Um cartão de telefone, por favor** *oon kartaoon deh tehlehfohneh, por favor*
I have been cut off	**Caíu a chamada(P) linha(B)** *kah-eeoo ah shahmahdah(P) leenyah(B)*
I can't hear well	**Não se ouve bem** *naoon seh oh-ooveh behn*
May I speak to…?	**Posso falar com…?** *pohssoo fahlar kohn…?*
What is the prefix for United States / England?	**Qual é o prefixo da Estados Unidos / Inglaterra?** *kwahl eh oo prehfeeksoo dah ehshtahdosh ooneedosh / eenglahtehrrah?*
How much does it cost to phone…?	**Quanto custa telefonar para…?** *kwahntoo kooshtah tehlehfoonar pahrah…?*

Excuse me, I have the wrong number

Desculpe, é engano
deshkoolpeh, eh ehngahnoo

I'd like to call collect

A despesa é a carico do destinatário
ah deshpehzah eh ah kahreekoo doo desteenahtaree-oo

YOU MAY BE TOLD/ASKED: ——————————

Com quem quer falar?
kohn kehn ker fahlar?

To whom do you wish to speak?

É impedido(P) ocupado(B)
eh eempehdeedoo(P) ohkoopahdoo(B)

The line is engaged

Não está
naoon shtah

He/She isn't here

Não responde ninguém
naoon respohndeh neengehn

There is no answer

Quem fala?
kehn fahlah?

Who is speaking?

Quer deixar um recado?
kehr deh-eeshar oon rehkahdoo?

Do you want to leave a message?

Tente mais tarde
tehnteh mah-eesh tardeh

Try again later

Um momento. Espere na linha
oon moomentoo. shpehreh nah leenyah

One moment. Hold the line

What time is it?	**Que horas são?** *keh orash saoon?*
It is noon	**É meio dia** *eh meh-eeoo dee-ah*
It is midnight	**É meia noite** *eh meh-eeah noh-eeteh*
It is ...	**São...** *saoon ...*
7.00	**sete** *sehteh*
8.05	**oito e cinco** *oh-eetoo ee seenkoo*
9.40	**nove e quarenta / dez menos vinte** *nohveh ee kwahrentah /* *desh mehnoosh veenteh*
10.15	**dez e quinze / dez e um quarto** *desh ee keenzeh / desh ee oon kwartoo*
11.20	**onze e vinte** *ohnzeh ee veenteh*
12.30	**meio dia e meia, doze e trinta** *meh-eeoo dee-ah ee meh-eeah,* *dohze ee treentah*
12.00	**é meio dia** *eh meh-eeoo deeah*
24.00	**é meia noite** *eh meh-eeah noh-eeteh*

It is nine A.M. / P.M.	**São nove horas da manhã/da noite** _saoon nohveh orash dah manyah / dah noh-eeteh_
It is four A.M. / P.M.	**São quatro horas da manhã/da tarde** _saoon kwahtroo orash dah manyah / dah tarde_
What time do the shops open / close?	**A que horas abrem/fecham as lojas?** _ah keh orash ahbrehn / fehshahn ash lohjash?_
What time does the restaurant open / close?	**A que horas abre/fecha o restaurante?** _ah keh orash ahbreh / fehshah oo restah-oorahnteh?_
What time does the film start / finish?	**A que horas começa/acaba o filme?** _ah keh orash koomesah / ahkahbah oo feelmeh?_
What time does the plane / bus leave?	**A que horas é o avião/o autocarro(P) ônibus(B)?** _ah keh orash eh oo ahvee-aoon / oo ah-ootohkaroo (P) / ohneeboosh (B)?_
It is late/ early	**É atrasado/adiantado** _eh ahtrahzahdoo / ahdyahntahdoo_
It's too early / late	**É cedo / tarde demais** _eh sehdoo / tardeh dehmah-eesh_
How long does it take to get there?	**Quanto tempo se demora para chegar lá?** _kwahntoo tehmpoo seh dehmohrah pahrah shehgar lah?_
We have arrived early / late	**Chegamos cedo / tarde** _shehgahmoosh sehdoo / tardeh_

A little more	**Mais um bocado(P)** **mais um pouquinho(B)** *mah-eesh oon bookahdoo (P) mah-eesh oon poh-ookeenyoo*
Two kilos of …	**Dois quilos/kilos de…** *doh-eesh keelohs deh …*
It is long / short	**É comprido/curto** *eh kohmpreedoo / koortoo*
It is a lot / a little	**É muito/pouco** *eh moo-eentoo / poh-ookoo*
Half a liter of …	**Meio litro de…** *mehyoo leetroo deh ……*
Three hundred grams of …	**Trezentas gramas de…** *trehzehntash grahmash deh…*
A hundred grams of…	**Cem gramas de…** *sehn grahmash deh…*
A kilo of …	**Um quilo/kilo de…** *oon keeloo deh…*
A glass of …	**Um vidrinho de…** *oon veedreenyoo deh…*
A dozen	**Uma dúzia** *oomah doozyah*
A slice	**Uma fatia** *oomah fahtee-ah*
A portion	**Uma porção** *oomah porsaoon*
A can	**Uma caixa** *oomah kah-eeshah*

What's the weather like today?	**Como é o tempo hoje?** *kohmoo eh oo tehmpoo ohjeh?*
What was the weather like yesterday?	**Como era o tempo ontem?** *kohmoo ehrah oo tehmpoo ontehn?*
What's the temperature today?	**Quantos graus fazem(P) estão(B)?** *kwahntoosh grah-oosh fahzen(P) eeshtaoon(B)?*
Will there be a storm?	**Vai fazer um temporal?** *vah-ee fahzer oon tehmpoohrahl?*
Will it be a nice day tomorrow?	**Amanhã vai fazer bom tempo?** *ahmahnyah vah-ee fahzer bohn tehmpoo?*
It's hot/cold	**Faz(P) Está(B) calor/frio** *fash(P) tah(B) kahlor/free-oo*
It's about 26°	**Fazem mais ou menos vinte e seis graus** *fahzen mah-eesh oh-oo mehnoosh veenteh ee seh-eesh grah-oosh*
The weather is good/bad today	**Hoje faz(P) está(B) bom/mau tempo** *ohjeh fash(P) tah(B) bohn/mah-oo tehmpoo*
It is windy	**Faz(P) Está(B) vento** *fash(P) tah(B) vehntoo*
It is raining	**Chove** *shohveh*

GASTRONOMIC
DICTIONARY

about ao redor *ah-oo rehdor*
  about ten aproximadamente
  às dez horas
  ahprohseemahdahmehnteh
  ash desh ohrash
above em cima *ehn seemah*
accept, to aceitar *ahsseh-*
  eetar
accident acidente
  aseedehnteh
ache dor *dor;* **headache** dor
  de cabeça *dor deh*
  kahbehsah; **stomachache**
  dor de barriga *dor deh*
  bareegah; **toothache** dor de
  dente *dor deh dehnteh;*
  stomachache dor de
  estômago *dor deh*
  shtomahgoo
acid ácido *ahseedoo*
address morada (P)
  moorahdah endereço (B)
  ehnderesoo
adhesive tape fita adesiva (P)
  feetah ahdehzeevah durex
  (B) *doorehks*
adjust, to arranjar *ahrahnjar*
adult adulto *adooltoo*
after depois *dehpoh-eesh*
afternoon tarde *tardeh*
aftershave loção pós-barba
  loossaoon posh-barbah
again de novo *deh nohvoo*
age idade *eedahdeh*

ahead em frente *ehn frehnteh*
air ar *ar;* **air conditioning** ar
  condicionado *ar*
  kohndeessyoonahdoo
airplane avião *ahvee-aoon*
airport aeroporto *ah-*
  ehrohpohrtoo
alcoholic alcoólico *alkoo-*
  ohleekoo
alight, lit aceso *ahssehzoo*
all todo *tohdoo*
allergy alergia *ahlerdjee-ah*
almond amêndoa
  ahmehndoo-ah
almost quase *kwahzeh*
also também *tahmbehn*
always sempre *sehmpreh*
ambulance ambulância
  amboolahnsee-ah
amusing engraçado
  ehngrahsahdoo
anchovy anchova
  ahnshohvah
and e *eh*
animal animal *ahneemahl*
aniseed anis *ahneesh*
answer, to responder
  reshpohnder
antibiotic antibiótico
  ahnteebee-ohteekoo
any algum *ahlgoon*
any qualquer *kwahlker*
apartment apartamento
  ahpartahmehntoo

aperitif aperitivo
 ahpehree<u>tee</u>voo
appetite apetite _ahpeh<u>tee</u>teh_
apple maçã _mah<u>sah</u>_; **quince
 apple** marmelo _mar<u>meh</u>loo_
appointment encontro
 ehn<u>koh</u>ntroo
apricot damasco
 dah<u>mah</u>shkoo
April abril _a<u>breel</u>_
aquavitae aguardente (P)
 ahgwahr<u>deh</u>nteh cachaça
 (B) _kah<u>shah</u>ssah_
arm braço _b<u>rah</u>ssoo_
armchair poltrona
 pohlt<u>roh</u>nah
aroma aroma _a<u>roh</u>mah_
arrive to chegar _sheh<u>gar</u>_
artichoke alcachofra
 ahlkah<u>sho</u>frah
ashtray cinzeiro _seen<u>seh</u>-
 eeroo_
asparagus espargos
 eesh<u>par</u>goosh
aspirin aspirina
 ahspee<u>ree</u>nah
assignment encomenda
 ehnkoo<u>meh</u>ndah
at least ao menos _ah-oo
 <u>meh</u>noosh_
at, to a, em _ah, ehn_ **I'm at
 home** estou em casa _sh<u>toh</u>-
 oo ehn <u>kah</u>zah_
attack ataque _ah<u>tah</u>keh_

attention atenção
 ahtehnss<u>aoo</u>n
au gratin gratinado
 grahteen<u>ah</u>doo
August agosto _ah<u>gosh</u>too_
authentic autêntico _ah-
 oo<u>tehn</u>teekoo_
automatic automático _ah-
 ootoom<u>ah</u>teekoo_
autumn outono _oh-oot<u>oh</u>noo_
average médio _<u>meh</u>dee-oo_
avocado abacate
 ahbah<u>kah</u>tchee
avoid, to evitar _ehvee<u>tar</u>_

baby-sitter babá _bah<u>bah</u>_
back (of the body) costas
 <u>kosh</u>tash
back atrás _ah<u>trash</u>_
backpack mochila
 moosh<u>ee</u>lah
bacon toucinho (P) _toh-
 oo<u>see</u>nyoh_ bacon (B)
 be<u>hkohn</u> **smoked b.** bacon
 defumado _behkohn
 dehfoom<u>ah</u>doo_
bacon toucinho (P) _toh-
 oo<u>see</u>nyoo_ bacon(B) _beh-
 ee<u>kohn</u>_
bad (of food) estragado (P)
 shtrahg<u>ah</u>doo podre (B)
 <u>poh</u>dreh; **(of weather)** mau
 mah-oo; **(of news)** má _mah_
badly mal _mal_

bag bolsa *bohlsah*
balance equilíbrio *ehkeeleebree-oo*
balcony varanda *varahnda*
banana banana *bahnahnah*
bandage atadura (P) *ahtahdoorah* gaze (B) *gahzeh*
band-aid penso (P) *pehnsoo* band-aid (B) *bahnd-eh-eed*
bank banco *bahnkoo*
  commercial b. comercial *koomehrsee-ahl* **investment b.** de investimentos *deh eenveshteemehntoosh*
barber barbeiro *barbeh-eeroo*
barley cevada *sehvahdah*
barman barman *barman*
basic fundamental *foondahmehntahl*
basil manjericão *mahnjehreekaoon*
bathroom banho *bahnyoo*
batter pastel *pashtehl*
bay (leaf) louro *loh-ooroh*
be able, to poder *pooder*
be born, to nascer *nashser*
be, to ser *ser* (see "Grammar")
beach praia *prah-ee-ah*
bean feijão *feh-eejaoon*
beard barba *barbah*
because já que *jah keh*

because porque *porkeh*
bechamel sauce besciamel *beshamehl*
become, to transformar-se *transhfoormar-seh*
bed cama *kahmah*
beef boi *boh-ee*
beer cerveja *chervehjah*
beetroot beterraba *behtehrahbah*
begin, to começar *koomesar*
beginning início *eeneesyoo*
behind atrás *ahtrash*
bell pepper pimentão *peemehntaoon*
belt cinto *seentoo* **safety b.** de segurança *deh sehgoorahnsah*
beside ao lado *ah-oo lahdoo*
better melhor *mehlyor*
better melhor *mehlyor*
between entre *ehntreh*
bicycle bicicleta *beesseeklehtah*
big grosso *grohssoo*
bikini fato de banho (P) *fahtoo deh bahnyoo* bikini (B)
bill conta *kohntah*
binoculars binóculo *beenohkooloo*
bird pássaro *pahsahroo*
birthday aniversário *ahneeversaree-oo*

biscuit biscoito *beeshkoh-eetoo*
bite mordida *moordeedah*
bitter amargo *ahmargoo*
black preto *prehtoo*
blade lâmina (P) *lahmeenah* gillette (B) *jeeleht*
blanket cobertor *koobertor*
bleach lixívia (P) *leesheevyah* água sanitária (B) *ahgwah sahneetaree-ah*
blocked bloqueado *blookeh-ahdoo*
blood sangue *sangeh*
blue azul *ahzool*
board and lodging pensão *pehnsaoon*
boat barco *barkoo*
boil, to ferver *fervehr*
boiled cozido *koozeedoo*
boiling fervendo *fervehndoo*
bone osso *ohsoh*
book livre *leevreh*
book livro *leevroo*
bookshop livraria *leevraree-ah*
boring chato *shahtoo*
both ambos *ahnbosh*
bottle garrafa *gahrahfah*
bottle opener abre garrafas *ahbreh gahrahfash*
bottled engarrafado *ehngarahfahdoo*
bovine bovino *booveenoo*

boy rapaz (P) *rahpash* garoto (B) *garohtoh*
bra soutien *sootyahn*
bracelet pulseira *poolseh-eerah*
brain cérebro *sehrehbroo*
brake travão (P) *trahvaoon* freio (B) *freh-eeyoo*
bread pão *paoon*
breadcrumbs pão ralado *paoon raladoo*
breaded empanado *ehnpahnahdoo*
breadshop padaria *pahdaree-ah*
breakfast pequeno-almoço (P) *pekehnoo ahlmohsoo* café-da-manhã (B) *kahfeh dah mahnyah* **in the room** no quarto *noo kwartoo*
breeding (of animal) de criação *deh kree-ahssaoon*
brioche croissant *kroh-ahssahn*
broad bean fava *fahvah*
broccoli brócolis *brohkooleesh*
broken partido (P) *parteedoo* quebrado (B) *kehbrahdoo*
broth caldo *kahldoo*
brother irmão *eermaoon*
brown marrom *marohn*
Brussels sprouts couve de bruxelas *kohooveh deh*

broosh-ehlash
buffet buffet *boofeh*
building prédio *prehdee-oo*
bulb (light b.) lâmpada *lahnpahdah*
burn, to queimar *keh-eemar*
burnt queimado *keh-eemahdoo*
bus autocarro (P) *ah-ootohkaroo* ônibus (B) *ohneeboosh*
business negócio *nehgohssyoo*
but mas *mash*
butcher's talho (P) *tahlyoo* açougue (B) *ahssoh-oogeh*
butter manteiga *mahnteh-eegah*
buttered amanteigado *ahmahnteh-eegahdoo*
butterfly borboleta *boorboolehtah*
button botão *bootaoon*
buy, to comprar *kohmprar*

cabbage couve *koh-ooveh*
cable car teleférico (P) *tehlehfereekoo* bondinho (B) *bohndjeenyoo*
café bar *bar*
cake bolo *bohloo*
call chamada (P) *shahmahdah* ligação (B) *leegahsaoon*

call, to chamar *shahmar*
calm calmo *kahlmoo;* tranquilo *trahnkeeloo*
calorie calorias *kalkooree-ash*
camera máquina fotográfica *mahkeenah fohtohgrafeekah*
camomile camomila *kahmoomeelah*
camp site parque de campismo (P) *parkeh deh kahmpeeshmoo* acampamento (B) *ahkahmpahmehntoo*
camp, to acampar *ahkahmpar*
can (e.g. of coke etc.) lata *lahtah*
can opener abre latas *ahbreh lahtash*
canal canal *kahnahl*
canapé canapé *kahnahpeh*
cancel, to cancelar *kahnchehlar;* negar *nehgar*
candle vela *vehlah*
candy rebuçado (P) *rehboosahdoo* bala (B) *bahlah*
canoe canoa *kahnoh-ah*
cap (for shower etc.) touca de banho *toh-ookah deh bahnyoo*
capers alcaparras *ahlkahparash*
car carro *karoo*

car park estacionamento _shtassyoonahmehntoo_
carafe garrafa _garahfah_
carburettor carburador _karboorahdor_
carpet tapete _tahpehteh_
carriage vagão _vagaoon_
carrot cenoura _sehnoh-oorah_
carry, to levar _lehvar_
cashier caixa _kah-eeshah_
casino cassino _kahseenoo_
castle castelo _kashtehloo_
Catholic católico _kahtohleekoo_
cauliflower couve-flor _koh-ooveh flor_
celery aipo _ah-eepoh_
center centro _sehntroo_
centimeter centímetro _sehnteemehtroo_
central central _sehntrahl_
ceramics cerâmica _sehrahmeekah_
cereal cereal _sehreh-ahl_
certificate certificado, certidão _serteefeekahdoo, serteedaoon_ birth **c.** de nascimento _deh nashsseemehntoo_ marriage **c.** de casamento _deh kahzahmehntoo_
chair cadeira _kahdeh-eerah_
champagne champagne _shahmpahnyeh_

change (coins) resto, troco _reshtoo, trohkoo_
change, to (something) mudar _moodar_; (money) trocar _trookar_
chapel capela _kahpehlah_
cheap barato _bahrahtoo_
check cheque _shehkeh_
check, to verificar _vehreefeekar_
checkbook livro de cheques (P) _leevroo deh shekesh_ talão de cheques (B) _tahlaoon djee shekeesh_
cheerfulness alegria _ahlehgree-ah_
cheese queijo _keh-eejoo_
cherry cereja _sehrehjah_
chest (breast) peito _peh-eetoo_
chestnut castanha _kastahnyah_
chew, to mastigar _mashteegar_
chichory chicória _sheekohree-ah_
chicken frango _frahngoo_
chickpeas grão _graoon_
chicory chicória _sheekoree-ah_
child menino _mehneenoo_
chili piripiri (P) _peereepeeree_ pimenta malagueta (B) _peemehntah mahlahgehtah_
chin queixo _keh-eeshoo_

chocolate chocolate
Christmas natal *nahtahl*
church igreja *eegrehjar*
cider sidra *seedrah*
cigar charuto *shrootoo*
cigarette cigarro *seegahroo*
cemetery cemitério
  sehmeetehree-oo
cinema cinema *seenehmah*
cinnamon canela *kahnehlah*
citrus fruit frutas cítricas
  frootash seetreekash
city cidade *seedahdeh*
city map mapa das estradas
  mahpah dash shtrahdash
clams mexilhões
  mesheelyoh-eens
clean limpo *leempoo*
clean, to limpar *leempar*
climb, to subir *soobeer*
clock, watch (wrist w.)
  relógio *rehlohjoo*
close, to fechar *feshar*
closed fechado *feshahdoo*
cloud nuvem *noovehn*
cloudy nublado *nooblahdoo*
club clube *kloobeh*
coach (for tourists) autocarro
  (P) *ah-ootokahroo* ônibus
  (B) *ohneeboosh*
coast custa *kooshtah*
coat-hanger cabide
  kahbeedeh
cockerel galeto *gahlehtoo*

cocoa cacau *kahkah-oo*
coconut côco *kohkoo*
coconut water água de côco
  ahgwah djee kohkoo
  coconut milk leite de côco
  leh-eeteh djee kohkoo
  grated coconut côco ralado
  kohkoo rahlahdoo
cod (dried) bacalhau
  bahkahlyee-ah-oo
coffee café *kahfeh*
coffee with milk café com
  leite *kahfeh kohn leh-eeteh*
coin moeda *moo-ehdah*
cold frio *free-oo*
color cor *kor*
comb pente *pehnteh*
come, to vir *veer*
comfortable confortável
  kohnfoortahvehl
complaint reclamação
  rehklahmahsaoon
compulsory obrigatório
  ohbreegahtohree-oo
computer computador
  kohmpootahdor
confirm, to confirmar
  kohnfeermar
congratulations! parabéns!
  parahbensh!
consulate consulado
  kohnsoolahdoo
contact contato *kohntahtoo*
contraceptive

anticoncepcional
ahnteekonnsehpsyohnahl
cook cozinheiro
koozeenyeh-eeroo
cookshop churrascaria
shoorashkahree-ah
cook, to cozer *koozer*
cool, to resfriar *rehsfree-ar*
copy, to copiar *koopee-ar*
coriander coentro *koo-
ehntroo*
corkscrew abre-rolhas (P)
ahbreh rohlyash abre-
garrafa (B) *ahbreh garahfah*
cosmetics cosméticos
koshmehteekoosh
cost, to custar *kooshtar*
cotton algodão *ahlgodaoon*
cough tosse *tohseh*
country(side) campo
kahmpoo
country país *pah-eesh*
couple cópia *kohpee-ah*
crab caranguejo
kahrahngehjoo
crash helmet capacete
kahpahsehteh
cream creme *krehmeh;* nata
nahtah
credit card cartão de crédito
kartaoon deh krehdeetoo
crowded cheio *sheh-ee-oo*
cruise cruzeiro marítimo
kroozeh-eeroo mareeteemoo

cucumber pepino *pehpeenoo*
cup chávena (P) *shahvehnah*
xícara (B) *sheekarah*
currants groselha
groozehlyah
currency cotação
kootahsaoon
cushion almofada
ahlmoofahdah
customer cliente *klee-ehnteh*
customs alfândega
ahlfahndehgah
cut corte *korteh*
cut, to cortar *koortar*
cutlet costoleta
kooshtoolehtah
cycling ciclismo
seekleeshmoo

daily diário *dee-areeyoo*
damage dano, defeito
dahnoo, dehfeh-eetoo
damp úmido *oomeedoo*
dance dança *dahnsa*
dance, to dançar *dahnsar*
dangerous perigoso
pereegohzoo
dark escuro *shkooroo*
date data *dahtah* **arrival d.**
de chegada *deh
shehgahdah* **departure d.** de
partida *deh parteedah*
day dia *dee-ah*
debit, to (someone for

something) pôr na conta de *por nah kohntah deh*

decaffeinated descafeinado *deshkahfeh-eenahdoo*

December dezembro *dehzehmbroo*

declare, to declarar *dehklarar*

decorated decorado *dehkoorahdoo*

decoration decoração *dehkoorahssaoon*

decrease, to diminuir *deemeenoo-eer*

deep profundo *proofoondoo*

delay atraso *ahtrahzoo*

delicious delicioso (P) *dehleesee-ohzoo* gostoso (B) *goshtoh-zoo*

dentex pargo *pargoo*

dentist dentista *dehnteeshtah*

denture dentadura *dehntahdoorah*

deny, to negar *nehgar*

deodorant desodorizante (P) *dezodooreezahnteh* desodorante (B) *dehzohdohrahntchee*

departure partida *parteedah*

deposit, to depositar *dehpoozeetar*

dessert sobremesa *soobrehmehzah*

destiny destino *deshteenoo*

details detalhes *dehtahlyesh*

detergent detergente *dehterjehnteh*

develop, to desenvolver *dehzehnvohlver*

diabetic diabético *dee-ahbehtikoo*

dialogue diálogo *dee-ahloogoo*

diamond diamante *dee-ahmahnteh*

diaper fralda *frahldah*

diarrhea diarréia *dee-areh-yah*

diary diário *dee-ahree-oo*

dictionary dicionário *deesyoonahree-oo*

diesel oil gasólio *gahzohlyoo*

diet alimentação *ahleemehntahssaoon;* dieta *dee-ehtah*

different diferente *deefehrehnteh;* diverso *deeversoo*

difficult difícil *deefeeseel*

digestive digestivo *deedjeshteevoo*

dining room sala de jantar *sahlah deh jahntar*

direct direto *deerehtoo*

direction direção *deerehsaoon*

director diretor *deerehtor*

dirty sujo *soojoo*

disabled person deficiente físico *defeesyehnteh feezeekoo*

discotheque discoteca *deeshkootekah*

discount desconto *deshkohntoo*

dishwasher máquina de lavar louça *mahkeenah deh lahvar loh-oossah*

disinfectant desinfetante *dehzeenfehtahnteh*

disk disco *deeshkoo* **CD** *sehdeh*

distance distância *deeshtahnsee-ah*

distrust, to desconfiar *dehkohnfee-ar*

disturb, to incomodar *eenkoomoodar*

diversion desvio *deshvyoo*

divide, to dividir *deeveedeer*

divorced divorciado *deevorsee-ahdoo*

do, to (make) fazer *fahzer*

doctor médico *mehdeekoo*

document documento *dookoomehntoo*

dog cão (P) *kaoon* cachorro (B) *kashoroo*

doll boneca *boonehkah*

dollar dólar *dohlar*

door porta *portah*

double duplo *dooploo*

down em baixo *ehn bah-eeshoo*

down there lá em baixo *lah ehn bah-eeshoo*

drama drama *drahmah*

dress, to vestir *veshteer*

dressed roupa *roh-oopah*

dressing (sauce etc.) tempero *tehmpehroo*

dried sausage carnes salgadas *karnesh sahlgahdash*

drink bebida *behbeedah*

drink, to beber *behbehr*

drive, to guiar, conduzir (P) *gee-ar, kohndoozeer* dirigir (B) *deereejeer*

driver condutor (P) *kohndootor* motorista (B) *mohtohreeshtah*

driving licence carta de condução (P) *kartah deh kohndoosaoon* carteira de motorista (B) *karteh-eerah djee mohtoreeshtah*

drumstick coxa de frango *koshah deh frahngoo*

drunk bêbado *behbahdoo*

dry cleaner's limpeza a seco *leempehzah ah sehkoo*

dry seco *sehkoo*

duck pato *pahtoo*

dune duna *doonah*

duration duração
doorahss<u>aa</u>oon
during durante _doo<u>rah</u>nteh_
dust pó _p<u>oh</u>_

each cada _k<u>ah</u>dah_
each one cada um _k<u>ah</u>dah oon_
ear orelha _or<u>eh</u>lyah_
early cedo _s<u>eh</u>doo_
earring brinco _br<u>een</u>koo_
earth terra _t<u>eh</u>rah_
East leste _l<u>esh</u>teh_
Easter páscoa _p<u>ash</u>koo-ah_
easy fácil _f<u>ah</u>sseel_
eat, to comer _koom<u>er</u>_
eel enguia _ehn<u>gee</u>-ah_
egg ovo _ohv<u>oo</u>_
egg yolk gema de ovo _j<u>eh</u>mah deh <u>oh</u>voo_
eggplant beringela _bereen<u>jeh</u>lah_
eggwhite clara do ovo _kl<u>ah</u>rah doo <u>oh</u>voo_
egoism egoísmo _eegoo-<u>ee</u>shmoo_
elastic elástico _eel<u>ash</u>teekoo_
electric elétrico _ehl<u>eh</u>treekoo_
electricity eletricidade _ehlehtreeseed<u>ah</u>dheh_
elegant elegante _ehleh<u>gah</u>nteh_
elevator elevador _ehlehvahd<u>oh</u>r_

embark embarcar _ehnbark<u>ar</u>_
embarrassment embaraço _ehnbar<u>ah</u>soo_
embassy embaixada _ehmbah-eesh<u>ah</u>dah_
emergency emergência _ehmerdj<u>eh</u>nsee-ah_
empire império _eenp<u>eh</u>ree-oo_
empty vazio _vahzy<u>oo</u>_
end fim _feen_
energy energia _ehner<u>jee</u>-ah_
engine motor _moot<u>or</u>_
enjoy, to aceitar _ahsseh-eet<u>ar</u>_
enough suficiente _soofeessee-<u>eh</u>nteh_
enquiry pesquisa _peshk<u>ee</u>zah_
enter, to entrar _ehntr<u>ar</u>_
entertainment divertimento _deeverteem<u>eh</u>ntoo_
entrance entrada _ehntr<u>ah</u>dah_
envelope envelope _ehnveh<u>loh</u>peh_
envy inveja _eenv<u>eh</u>jah_
error erro _<u>e</u>roo_
escalope escalope _shkah<u>loh</u>peh_
escape fuga _f<u>oo</u>ga_
Europe Europa _eh-oor<u>oh</u>pah_
event evento _ehv<u>eh</u>ntoo_
evident evidente _ehveed<u>eh</u>nteh_
exam exame _ehs<u>ah</u>meh_
examine, to examinar _ehsahmeen<u>ar</u>_

excellent excelente *eh-eesheh<u>leh</u>nteh*
except exceto *eh-eesh<u>eh</u>too*
excess excesso *eh-eesh<u>es</u>soo*
exciting excitante *eh-eesheet<u>ah</u>nteh*
excursion excursão *eh-eeshkoors<u>ao</u>on*
exit saída *sah-<u>ee</u>dah*
expense despesa *deshp<u>eh</u>zah*
expensive caro *k<u>ar</u>oo*
expert perito *peh<u>ree</u>too*
explosion explosão *eh-eeshploos<u>ao</u>on*
express expresso *eh-eeshp<u>reh</u>soo*
extend, to alargar *ahlarg<u>ar</u>*
external externo *eh-eesht<u>er</u>noo*
extinguisher extintor de incêndio *eh-eeshteent<u>or</u> deh eens<u>eh</u>ndyoo*
extract extrato *eh-eesht<u>rah</u>too*
extremity extremidade *eh-eeshtrehmeed<u>ah</u>deh*
eye olho *<u>oh</u>lyoo*

fabric tecido *teh<u>see</u>doo*
facing em frente *ehn f<u>reh</u>nteh*
faint, to desmaiar *deshmah-ee-a<u>r</u>*
fair feira *f<u>eh</u>-eerah*
fall, to cair *kah-<u>ee</u>r*

familiar familiar *fahmeely<u>ar</u>*
family família *fahm<u>ee</u>lyah*
famous famoso *fahm<u>oh</u>zoo*
fan ventoinha (P) *vehntoo-<u>ee</u>nyah* ventilador (B) *vehnteelahd<u>or</u>*
far longe *l<u>oh</u>njeh*
farm quinta (P) *k<u>ee</u>ntah* sítio (B) *s<u>ee</u>tyoo*
fat gordo *g<u>or</u>doo*
father pai *p<u>ah</u>-ee*
favor favor *fahv<u>or</u>*
favorite preferido *prehfeh<u>ree</u>doo*
fever febre *f<u>eh</u>breh*
fiancé namorado *nahmoor<u>ah</u>doo*
fig figo *f<u>ee</u>goo* **dried figs** figos secos *f<u>ee</u>goosh s<u>eh</u>koosh*
fill, to encher *ehnsh<u>er</u>*
filling (tooth) obturação *ohbtoorahs<u>ao</u>on*
film filme *f<u>ee</u>lmeh*
filter filtro *f<u>ee</u>ltroo*
fine (noun) multa *m<u>oo</u>ltah*
finish, to acabar *ahkahb<u>ar</u>*
fire fogo *f<u>oh</u>goo*
fire plug hidratante *eedraht<u>ah</u>nteh*
fireman bombeiro *bohnb<u>eh</u>-eeroo*
first aid pronto socorro *pr<u>oh</u>ntoo sook<u>oh</u>roo*

first class primeira classe *preemeh-eerah klahseh*
first primeiro *preemeh-eeroo*
fish peixe *peh-eesheh*
fish, to pescar *peshkar*
fizzy com gás *kohn gash*
flame chama *shahmah*
flask fracasso *frahkahsoo*
flavor sabor *sahbor*
flight vôo *voh-oo*
floor (of a building) andar *ahndar*
floor chão *shaoon*
flour farinha *fareenyah*
flower flor *flor*
fly mosca *moshkah*
food alimento *ahleemehntoo*; comida *koomeedah*
food poisoning intoxicação alimentar *eentokseekahsaoon ahleemehntar*
for para *parah*
foreigner estrangeiro *shtrahnjeh-eeroo*
forest floresta *flooreshtah*
forget, to esquecer *shkeser*
fork garfo *garfoo*
fountain fonte *fohnteh*
four quatro *kwatroo*
fragile frágil *frahjeel*
fragrance perfume *perfoomeh*

France França *frahnsah*
frankfurter salsicha *sahlseeshah*
free (no payment) grátis *grahteesh*
freeway auto-estrada *ah-ootoh-shtrahdah*
French fries batatas fritas *bahtahtash freetash*
fresh fresco *freshkoo*
Friday sexta-feira *seshtah feh-eerah*
fried frito *freetoo*
friend amigo *ahmeegoo*
frog rã *rah*
frontier fronteira *frohnteh-eerah*
frost gelo *jehloo*
frozen congelado *kohnjehlahdoo*
fruit fruta *frootah*
fruit salad salada de frutas *sahlahdah deh frootash*
frying pan frigideira *freejeedeh-eerah*
full cheio *sheh-ee-oo*
furcoat casaco de peles *kazahkoo deh pehlesh*

gallery (art g.) galería de arte *gahleree-ah deh arteh*
game jogo *johgoo*
garage garagem *gahradjehn*
garbage lixo *leeshoo*

garden jardim *jardeen*
garlic alho *ahlyoo*
gas gás *gash*
gas pump bomba de gasolina *bohnbah deh gahzooleenah*
gas station bomba de gasolina (P) *bohmbah deh gahzooleenah* posto de gasolina (B) *poshtoo djee gahzohleenah*
gasoline gasolina *gahzooleena*
generally generalmente *jerahlmehnteh*
gentleman senhor *sehnyor*
genuine genuíno *jehnooeenoo*
get, to (a bus, etc.) subir *soobeer*
ginger gengibre *jehnjeebrah*
girl rapariga (P) *rahpareegah* garota (B) *garohtah*
glass copo *kohpoo*; vidro *veedroo*
glasses óculos *ohkooloosh*
gloves luvas *loovash*
glue cola *kohla*
go out, to sair *sah-eer*
go, to andar *ahndar*
God Deus *deh-oosh* **My God!** Meu Deus! *meh-oo deh-oosh*
gold ouro *oh-ooroh*

golden dourado *doh-oorahdoo*
golf golf
good bo (boa) *bohn (boh-ah)*
good afternoon boa tarde *boh-ah tardeh*
good evening boa noite *boh-ah noh-eeteh*
good morning bom dia *bohn dee-ah*
good night boa noite *boh-ah noh-eeteh*
goodbye! tchau *chah-oo*
goose ganso *gahnsoo*
gorgonzola gorgonzola *goorgonzohlah*
grain grão *graoon*
grams gramas *grahmash*
grape uva *oovah*
grapefruit toranja *toorahnjah*
grass erva *ervah*; **herbs** ervas aromáticas *ervash ahroomahteekahs*
gray cinza *seensah*
grease, to untar *oontar*
greasy gorduroso *goordoorohzoo*
green verde *verdeh*
green bean feijão-verde (P) *feh-eejaoon verdeh* vagem (B) *vahjehn*
grilled grelhada *grelyahdah*
grocer's mercearia (P)

mersyahree-ah drogaria (B) *drohgaree-ah*
group grupo *groopoo*
guarantee garantia *garahntee-ah*
guest hóspede *ohshpehdeh*
guide guia *gee-ah*

habit hábito *ahbeetoo*
hair cabelo *kahbehloo*
hairdresser cabeleireiro *kahbehleh-eereh-eeroo*
hairspray laca *lahkah*
half metade *mehtahdeh*
hall sala *sahlah*
ham presunto *prehzoontoo*
hand mão *maoon*
handkerchief (paper h.) lenço de papel *lehnsoo deh pahpehl*
happen, to acontecer *ahkohnteser*
happiness felicidade *fehleeseedahdeh*
happy feliz *fehleesh*
hard duro *dooroo*
hardware shop ferramenta *ferahmehntah*
hare lebre *lehbreh*
hat chapéu *shahpeh-oo*
have, to ter *tehr*
hazelnuts avelãs *ahvehlash*
he ele *ehleh* **she** ela *ehlah*
head cabeça *kahbehsah*

health saúde *sah-oodeh*
hear, to sentir *sehnteer*
heart coração *koorahssaoon*
heart attack enfarte *ehnfarteh*
heat, to aquecer *ahkehser*
heating aquecimento *akehseemehntoo*
helicopter helicóptero *ehleekohptehroo*
help ajuda *ahjoodah*
help, to ajudar *ahjoodar*
hemorrhoids hemorróidas *ehmohroh-eedash*
hen galinha *gahleenyah*
here aqui *ahkee*
herring arenque *arehnkeh*
hi! olá! (P) *ohlah* oi! (B) *oh-ee*
high alto *ahltoo*
hire, to alugar *ahloogar*
hit, to atingir *ahteenjeer*
hold, to pegar *pehgar*
hole buraco *boorahkoo*
holiday (vacation) férias *fehree-ash*
holiday (public) festa *feshtah*
holidays férias *feree-ash*
honey mel *mehl*
hors-d'oeuvre entrada *ehntrahdah*
horse cavalo *kahvahloo*
horse-, *adjective* hípico *eepeekoo*

hospital hospital *oshpeetahl*
hostess hospedeira (P)
ospehdeh-eerah aeromoça
(B) *ah-erohmohsah*
hot quente *kehnteh*
hot (spicy) picante
peekahnteh
hotel hotel *oh-tel*
hour hora *ohrah*
house casa *kahzah*
how como *koomoh*
how much quanto
kwahntoo
however porém *poorehm*
humility humildade
oomeeldahdeh
hunger fome *fohmeh*
hunting caça *kahssah*
hurry pressa *pressah*
husband marido *mareedoo*
hypertension hipertensão
eepertehnsaoon

I eu *eh-oo*
ice gelo *jehloo*
ice cream gelado (P)
jehlahdoo sorvete (B)
sorvehteh
ice cream parlor sorveteria
sorvehteree-ah
icy gelado *jehlahdoo*
idea idéia *eedeh-yah*
identical idêntico
eedehnteekoo

identity identidade
eedehnteedahdeh
idiom idioma *eedyohmah*
idol ídolo *eedooloo*
ill doente *doo-ehnteh*
illusion ilusão *eeloozaoon*
imagine imaginar
eemahjeenar
immediately imediatamente
eemehdee-ahtahmehnte
important importante
eenpoortahnteh
impossible impossível
eempooseevel
in (e.g. in a week) daqui a
dahkee ah; (e.g. in material)
de *deh*; (e.g. in Japan, in
China) no Japão, na China
noo jahpaoon, nah sheenah
in front em frente *ehn
frehnteh*
included incluído *eenkloo-
eedoo*
inconvenience incômodo
eenkohmoodoo
indicate, to indicar
eendeekar
indication indicação
eendeekasaoon
indigestion indigestão
eendeejeshtaoon
individual indivíduo
eendeeveedoo-oh
inferior inferior *eenferee-or*

influenza gripe *greepeh*
inform, to informar
 eenfoormar
information informação
 eenfoormahsaoon
ingredient ingrediente
 eengrehdyehnteh
injection injeção *eenjesaoon*
inn taberna *tahbernah*
innocent inocente
 eenoosehnteh
insect inseto *eensehto*
insert, to incluir *eenkloo-eer*
inside dentro *dehntroo*
instead ao invés *ah-oo*
 eenvesh
institute instituto
 eesteetootoo
instructor instrutor
 eenshtrootor
insulin insulina *eensooleenah*
intelligent inteligente
 eentehleejehnteh
interesting interessante
 eenteresahnteh
intermission intervalo
 eentervahloo
internal interno *eenternoo*
international internacional
 eenternasioonahl
interpreter intérprete
 eenterprehteh
interrupt interromper
 eenterohnper

intestine intestino
 eenteshteenoo
invitation convite
 kohnveeteh
invite, to convidar
 kohnveedar
invoice fatura *fahtoorah*
iron (for clothes) ferro de
 passar *feroo deh pahsar*
irritate, to irritar *eereetar*
island ilha *eelyah*
itch comichão
 koomeeshaoon
itinerary itinerário, roteiro
 eeteenerahryoo, rooteh-
 eeroo

jacket casaco *kahzahkoo*
jam marmelada
 marmehlahdah
January janeiro *jahneh-*
 eeroo
jelly gelatina *jehlahteenah*
jewel jóia *joh-eeyah*
jeweller's joalheria *joo-*
 ahlyeree-ah
joke anedota *ahnehdohtah*;
 brincadeira *breenkahdeh-*
 eerah
journey viagem *vee-ahjehn*
juice sumo (P) *seemoo* suco
 (B) *sookoh*
July julho *joolyoo*
June junho *joonyoo*

keep, to guardar *goo-ard<u>a</u>r*
key chave *sh<u>a</u>hveh*
kid (young goat) cabrito
  kahbr<u>ee</u>too
kidney rim *reen*; rojões
  rooj<u>oh</u>-eensh
kilo quilo, kilo *k<u>ee</u>loo*
kilometer quilometro,
  kilometro *keel<u>oh</u>mehtroo*
kind (adj.) gentil *jehnt<u>ee</u>l*
kiss beijo *b<u>e</u>h-eejoo*
kiss, to beijar *beh-eej<u>a</u>r*
kitchen cozinha *kooz<u>ee</u>nyah*
kiwi kiwi *k<u>ee</u>vee* (P) *k<u>ee</u>wee*
  (B)
knife faca *f<u>a</u>hkah*
know, to conhecer
  koonyes<u>e</u>r; saber *sahb<u>e</u>r*

label etiqueta *ehteek<u>e</u>htah*
laboratory laboratório
  lahbooraht<u>o</u>ree-oo
lace laço *l<u>a</u>hssoo*
ladle concha de servir
  k<u>o</u>hnshah deh serv<u>ee</u>r
lady senhora *sehny<u>o</u>rah*
lake lago *l<u>a</u>hgoo*
lamb cordeiro *koord<u>e</u>h-eeroo*
lamp candeeiro *kahndeh-<u>e</u>h-eeroo*; lume *l<u>oo</u>meh*
lard toucinho (P) *toh-oos<u>ee</u>nyoo* banha de porco
  (B) *b<u>a</u>hnyah djee p<u>o</u>rkoo*
large grande *gr<u>a</u>hndeh*

last último *<u>oo</u>lteemoo*
late é tarde *eh t<u>a</u>rdeh*
laundry lavanderia
  lahvahnder<u>ee</u>-ah
law lei *l<u>e</u>h-ee*
lawyer advogado
  ahdvoog<u>a</u>hdoo
laxative laxante *lash<u>a</u>hnteh*
learn, to aprender
  ahprehnd<u>e</u>r
leather couro *k<u>o</u>h-ooroo*
leave, to deixar *deh-eesh<u>a</u>r*;
  partir *part<u>ee</u>r*
leek alho-porro *<u>a</u>hlyoh
  pohr<u>o</u>h*
leg perna *p<u>e</u>rnah*
lemon limão *leem<u>a</u>oon*
lemonade limonada
  leemoon<u>a</u>hdah
lens lente *l<u>e</u>hnteh*
lentils lentilhas *lehnt<u>ee</u>lyash*
less menos *m<u>e</u>hnoosh*
lesson lição *leesa<u>o</u>on*
letter carta *k<u>a</u>rtah*
lettuce alface *ahlf<u>a</u>hseh*
library biblioteca *beeblee-oht<u>e</u>hkah* **national l.** b.
  nacional *b. nahssyoon<u>a</u>hl*
lid tampa *t<u>a</u>hmpah*
life vida *v<u>ee</u>dah*
life jacket colete salva-vidas
  kool<u>e</u>hteh s<u>a</u>hlvah v<u>ee</u>dash
light luz *l<u>oo</u>sh*
light (weight) leve *l<u>e</u>hveh*

light brown castanho *kastahnyoo*
light, to acender *ahssehnder*
  the water heater o aquecedor (P) *oo ahkessehdor* o boiler (B) *oo boh-eeler*
like, to gostar *gooshtar*
lipstick baton *bahtohn*
liqueur licor *leekor*
liquid for contact lenses soro para as lentes a contato *soroh parah ash lehntes ah kohntahtoo*
lira lira *leerah*
list lista *leeshtah*
listen, to ouvir *oh-ooveer*
liter litro *leetroo*
little pouco *poh-ookoo*
live, to viver *veever*
liver fígado *feegahdoo*
lobster lagosta *lahgoshta*; lavagante *lahvahgahnteh*
long comprido *kohmpreedoo*
long-distance call interurbano *eenteroorbahnoo*
look for, to procurar *prohkoorar*
look, to olhar *ohlyar*
lose, to perder *perder*
lotion loção *loosaoon*
love, to amar *ahmar*
low baixo *bah-eeshoo*

luggage bagagem *bahgahjehn*
lunch almoço *ahlmohsoo*
lupin seeds tremoços *trehmohsoosh*
luxury luxo *looshoo*

macaroni macarrão *mahkaraoon*
mackerel cavala *kahvahlah*
macrobiotic macrobiótico *mahkrohbee-ohteekoo*
magazine revista *rehveeshtah*
mail correio *kooreh-ee-oo*
mail, to pôr no correio *por noo kooreh-ee-oo*
main principal *preenseepahl*
maize milho *meelyoo*
make-up maquilhagem (P) *mahkeelyahjehn* maquiagem (B) *mahkee-ahjehn*
man homem *ohmehn*
manager executivo *ehsehkooteevoo*
map mapa *mahpah*
margarine margarina *margareenah*
market mercado *merkahdoo*
married casado *kahzahdoo*
mask máscara *mashkarah*
Mass missa *meesah*
match fósforo *foshfooroh*
mattress colchão *kohlshaoon*

May maio *mah-ee-oo*
mayonnaise maionese *mah-ee-ohnehzeh*
meal refeição *rehfeh-eesaoon*
means meio *meh-ee-oo*
meat carne *karneh*
meatball almôndega *ahlmohndehgah*
mechanic mecânico *mehkahneekoo*
medicine medicamento (P) *mehdeekahmehntoo* remédio (B) *rehmehdee-oo*
medlar nêspera *neshperah*
meet, to encontrar *ehnkohntrar*
melon melão *mehlaoon*
menstruation menstruação *mehnshtroo-ahsaoon*
menu menù *mehnoo;* ementa (P)*eemehntah;* cardápio (B) *kardahpyoo*
message recado *rehkahdoo*
metal metal *metahl*
migraine enxaqueca *ehnshahkehkah*
milk leite *leh-eeteh*
millimeter milímetro *meeleemetroo*
million milhão *meelyaoon*
mince (meat) carne picada (P) *karneh peekahdah* carne moída (B)*karneh moo-eedah*
minimum mínimo

meeneemoo
mint menta *mehntah*
minute minuto *meenootoo*
mirror espelho *shpehlyoo*
mistake engano *ehngahnoo*
misunderstanding equívoco *ehkeevookoo;* mal entendido *mal ehntehndeedoo*
mixed misto *meeshtoo*
mixture mistura *meeshtoorah*
modern moderno *moodernoo*
molluscs moluscos *mohlooshkoosh*
monastery mosteiro *mooshteh-eeroo*
Monday segunda-feira *sehgoondah feh-eerah*
money dinheiro *deenyeh-eeroo*
month mês *mesh*
monument monumento *mohnoomehntoo*
mood humor *oomor*
more mais *mah-eesh*
morning manhã *mahnyah*
mosquito mosquito *mooshkeetoo*
mother mãe *mah-een*
motorbike moto *mohtoh*
mountain montanha *mohntahnyah*
mourning luto *lootoo*

mouth boca *bohkah*
mozzarella cheese mussarela *moossarehlah*
much muito *moo-eentoo*
mullet tainha *tah-eenyah*; trilha *treelyah*
muscle músculo *mooshkooloo*
museum museu *moozeh-oo*
mushrooms cogumelos (P) *koogoomehloosh* champignon (B) *shampeenyohn*
music música *moozeekah*
mussel mexilhão *mesheelyeeaoon*
must dever *dehver*
mustard mostarda *mooshtardah*
mute mudo *moodoo*
mutton carneiro *karneh-eeroo*

nail (of metal) prego *prehgoo*
name nome *nohmeh*
narrow apertado *ahpertahdoo*
nation nação *nahssaoon*
national nacional *nasyoonahl*
nationality nacionalidade *nasyoonahleedahdeh*
natural natural *natoorahl*
naturalization naturalidade *nahtoorahlidahdeh*
nature natureza *nahtoorehzah*
nausea náusea *nah-oozeh-ah*
near perto *pertoo*
necessary necessário *nessessahryoo*
neck (of body) pescoço *peshkohsoo*; **(of shirt etc.)** gola *gohla*
necklace colar *koolar*
nectar néctar *nehktar*
needle (and thread) agulha (e linha) *ahgoolyah (ee leenyah)*
negative negativo *nehgahteevoo*
nerve nervo *nervoo*
nervous nervoso *nervohzoo*
nest ninho *neenyoo*
never nunca *noonkah* **never again** nunca mais *noonkah mah-eesh*
new novo *nohvoo*
New Year's Eve fim de ano (P) *feen deh ahnoo* revéillon (B) *rehveh-yohn*
newborn child recém-nascido *rehchehn nasheedoo*
news notícia *nooteesee-ah*
newspaper jornal *joornahl*
next próximo *prohseemoo*
nice (person) simpático *seempahteekoh*
night noite *noh-eeteh*

nightclub boite *booahteh;* lookal *notoornoo*

no não *naoon*

noble nobre *nohbreh*

nobody nenhum *nehnyoon*

noise barulho *baroolyoo*

non-alcoholic analcoólico *ahnahlkoo-ohleekoo*

non-smoker não-fumador *naoon foomahdor*

normal normal *normahl*

north norte *norteh*

nose nariz *nareesh*

nostalgia nostalgia *nooshtahljee-ah*

not even nem isso *nehn eessoo*

nothing nada *nahdah*

nourishing nutritivo *nootreeteevoo*

novel romance *roomahnseh*

novelty novidade *nooveedahdeh*

November novembro *noovehmbroo*

nude nú *noo*

number número *noomehroo*

nurse enfermeira *ehnfermeh-eerah*

nut noz *nosh*

nutmeg noz-moscada *nosh-mooshkahdah*

nutritious nutriente *nootree-ehnteh*

oats aveia *ahveh-eeyah*

obtain, to obtero *ohbter*

occupied ocupado *ohkoopahdoo*

October outubro *oh-ootoobroo*

octopus (octopus) polvo *pohlvoo*

odor cheiro *sheh-eeroo*

of de *deh*

offer, to oferecer *ohfehrehser*

office escritório *shkreetohree-oo*

often frequentemente *frehkwehntehmehnteh*

oil azeite *azeh-eeteh* **olive o.** azeite de oliva *azeh-eeteh deh ohleevah* **palm o.** azeite de dendê (B) *azeh-eeteh deh dehndeh* **seed o.** óleo *ohlyoo* **sun o.** bronzeador *brohnzeh-ahdor*

ointment pomada *poomahdah*

old velho *vehlyoo*

olive azeitona *azeh-eetohnah*

omelette omelete *ohmehlehteh*

on sobre, para cima *sohbreh, parah seemah*

one um *oon*

onion cebola *sehbohlah*
only sozinho *sohzeenyoo*
open aberto *ahbertoo*
open, to abrir *ahbreer*
opera ópera *ohperah*
orange (color) cor de laranja
  kor deh lahrahnjah
orange laranja *larahnjah*
orangeade laranjada (P)
  lahrahnjahdah suco de
  laranja (B) *sookoh djee
  lahrahnjah*
order, to pedir *pehdeer*
oregano orégano *orehganoo*
original original *oreejeenahl*
other outro *oh-ootroo*
out of order não funziona
  naoon foonsyohnah
outside fora *forah*
outskirts arredores (P)
  arehdohresh subúrbio (B)
  sooboorbyoo
oven forno *fornoo*
owner dono *dohnoo*
ox boi *boy*
oxygen oxigênio
  okseejehnyoo
oyster ostra *oshtrah*

pack pacote *pahkohteh*
packing embrulho
  ehnbroolyoo
paid pago *pahgoo*
pain dor *dor*

pain-killer analgésico
  ahnahljehzeekoo
painful doloroso
  dooloorohzoo
painting pintura *peentoorah*;
  quadro *kwahdroo*
pan panela *pahnehlah*
pancake rissól (P) *reessohl*
  pastel (B) *pashtehl*
panties calçinhas
  (B)*kahlseenyash*
pants calças *kahlssash*
paper papel *pahpehl*
parasol guarda-sol *guardah
  sohl*
pardon perdão *perdaoon*
parents pais *pah-eesh*
park parque *parkeh*
park, to estacionar
  shtassyoonah
parsley salsa *sahlsah*
part parte *parteh*
partridge perdiz *perdeesh*
pass (-card) passe (P) *pahseh*
  carteirinha (B) *karteh-
  eereenyah*
passenger passageiro
  pahsahjeh-eeroo
passion paixão *pah-eeshaoon*
passport passaporte
  pahsahporteh
pastry massa *mahsah* (for
  sweets) doce, bolinho
  dohseh, booleenyoo

paté paté *pahteh*
patience paciência *pahsee-ehnsee-ah*
paura medo *médu*
paw pata *pahtah*
pay, to pagar *pahgar*
payment pagamento *pahgahmehntoo*
peace paz *pahsh*
peach pêssego *pehsehgoo*
peak em cima *ehn seemah*
peanut amendoim *ahmehndoo-eem*
pear pêra *perah*
peas ervilhas *erveelyash*
peel, to descascar *deshkakar*
pen caneta *kanehtah*
pencil lápis *lahpeesh*
pensioner reformado (P) *rehfoormahdoo* aposentado (B) *ahpohzehntahdoo*
pepper pimenta *peemehntah*
perfect perfeito *perfeh-eetoo*
perhaps talvez *tahlvesh*
permanent permanente *permahnehnteh*
permission autorização *ahootohreezahsaoon*
person pessoa *pehsoh-ah*
pharmacy farmácia *farmahsyah*
photocopy fotocópia *fohtohkohpyah*

photograph fotografia *fohtohgrahfeeyah*
pickles pickles *peeklesh*
piece bocado (P) *bookahdoo* pedaço (B) *pehdahsoo*
pig, pork porco *porkoo*
pill pílula *peeloolah*
pineapple ananás (P) *ahnahnash* abacaxi (B) *ahbahkashee*
pink rosa *rohzah*
pipe cachimbo *kasheemboo*
pistachio pistache *peestasheh*
place lugar *loogar*
plant planta *plahntah*
plastic plástico *plashteekoo*
plate prato *prahtoo*
play, to jogar *joogar*
playing cards cartas *kartash*
plaza praça *prahsah*
plug tomada *toomahdah*
plum ameixa *ahmeh-eeshah*
plumber hidráulico *eedrahooleekoo*
police polícia *pooleesee-ah*
polluted poluído *pooloo-eedoo*
popular popular *pohpoolar*
pork suíno *soo-eenoo*
pork chop costoleta de porco *koo-shtooletah deh porcoo*
portrait retrato *rehtrahtoo*
Portugal Portugal *poortoogahl*

Portuguese português
poortoogesh
possible possível *pooseevehl*
postal order vale postal
vahleh pooshtahl
postcard cartão-postal
kartaoon pooshtahl
pot panela *pahnehlah*
potato batata *bahtahtah*
pram carrinho do bebê
kareenyoo doo behbeh
prawns shrimps camarões
kahmahroh-eens
prefer, to preferir *prehfehreer*
prefix (telephone) indicativo
(P) *eendeekahteevoo* prefixo
(B) *prehfeeksoo*
pregnant grávida *grahveedah*
prepare, to preparar
prehparar
present presente
prehzehnteh
preserved meats salame
sahlahmeh
pressure pressão *prehsaoon*
price preço *prehsoo*
price list lista de preços
leeshtah deh preshoosh
prick, to picar *peekar*
priest padre *pahdreh*
prision prisão *preezaoon*
private privado *preevahdoh*
probably provavelmente
prohvahvehlmehnteh

problem problema
prooblehmah
profession profissão
proofeesaoon
professor professor *proofesor*
program programa
proograhmah
pronounce, pronunciar
prohnoonsyar **How do you
pronounce ...?** como é que
se pronúncia...? *kohmoo eh
keh seh prohnoonsyah ...?*
public público *poobleekoo*
pudding pudim *poodeen*
puff pastry massa folhada
mahsah foolyahdah
pull, to puxar *pooshar*
pullover pulôver *poolohver*
pumpkin abóbora
ahbohboorah
put, to meter *mehter*
pyjamas pijama *peejahmah*

quail codorniz *koodoorneesh*
quality qualidade
kwahleedahdeh
quarter quarto *kwartoo*
question pergunta
pergoontah
questionnaire questionário
keshtyoonaree-oo
quick rápido *rahpeedoo*
quota prestação
preshtahsaoon

rabbit coelho *koo-ehlyoo*
radio rádio *rahdee-oo*
radish rabanete *rahbahnehteh*
rain chuva *shoovah*
rain, to chover *shoover*
raisin uvas passas *oovash pasash*
rapid rápido *rahpeedoo*
rare raro *raroo*
raw crú *kroo*
ready pronto *prohntoo*
receipt recibo *rehseeboo*
receive, to receber *rehsehber*
reception recepção *rehsehpsaoon*
recipe receita *rehseh-eetah*
refrigerator frigorífico (P) *freegooreefeekoo* geladeira (B) *jehlahdeh-eerah*
refund reembolso *reh-ehmbohlsoo*
region região *rehjee-aoon*
relative parente *parehnteh*
religion religião *rehleejee-aoon*
remain, to ficar *feekar*
remember, to lembrar *lehmbrar*
rent renda (P) *rehndah* aluguel (B) *ahloogeh-oo*
rent, to alugar *ahloogar*
reserve, to reservar *rehzervar*

reserved reservado *rehzervahdoo*
rest, to descansar *deskahnsar*
restaurant restaurante *reshtah-oorahnteh*
restroom toilette *too-ahleht*
return, to voltar *vohltar*
rice arroz *arosh*
ricotta cheese ricota *reekohtah*
right (direction) direita *deereh-eetah;* direito *deereh-eetoo;* certo *sertoo*
ring anel *ahnehl*
ripe maduro *mahdooroo*
risotto risoto *reezohtoo*
river rio *ree-oo*
roast assado *ahsahdoo*
rocket salad rúcula *rookoolah*
roll (cul.) rissól (P) *reessohl* salgadinho (B) *sahlgahdeenyoo*
room quarto *kwartoo*
rosé rosé *roseh*
rosemary rosmaninho *rohsmahneenyoo*
round redondo *rehdohndoo*
royal real *reh-ahl*
ruins ruínas *roo-eenash*
rum run *roon*

safe seguro *sehgooroo*
saffron açafrão *ahsahfraoon*

salad salada *sahlahdah*
salmon salmão *sahlmaoon*
salt sal *sahl*
salted biscuits salgadinhos *sahlgahdeenyoosh*
salted salgado *sahlgahdoo*
same igual *eegwahl*
sand areia *areh-ee-ah*
sandwich sandes (P) *sahndesh* sanduíche (B) *sahndweesheh*
sanitary towel penso higiênico (P) *pehnsoo eejee-ehneekoo* absorvente (B) *ahbsohrvehntchee*
Santa Claus pai natal (P) *pah-ee nahtahl* papai noel (B) *pahpah-ee noh-eh-oo*
sardine sardinha *sardeenyah*
Saturday sábado *sahbahdoo*
sauce molho *mohlyoo*
sauna sauna *sah-oonah*
sausage salsicha *salseesha*
say, to dizer *deezer*
scampi lagostim *lahgooshteen;* lagostins *lahgooshteensh*
school escola *shkohlah*
scissors tesoura *tezoh-oorah*
screwdriver chave de parafusos *shahveh deh parahfoozoosh*
sculpture escultura *shkooltoorah*

sea bream dourado *doh-oorahdoo*
sea mar *mar*
seafood fruto do mar *frootoo doo mar*
season estação *shtahsaoon*
second segundo *sehgoondoo*
see, to ver *ver*
seem, to parecer *parehcher*
sell, to vender *vehnder*
separate separado *sehparahdoo*
September setembro *setehmbru*
serious grave *grahveh*
service serviço *serveesoo*
set the table, to pôr a mesa *pohr ah mehzah*
shade sombra *sohmbrah*
she ela *ehlah*
sheet lençol *lehnsohl*
sherbet sorvete *sorvehteh*
ship navio *nahvee-oo*
shirt camisa *kahmeezah*
shoemaker sapateiro *sahpahteh-eeroo*
shop loja *lohjah*
shop window montra (P) *mohntrah* vitrine (B) *veetreeneh*
short curto *koortoo*
shoulder ombro *ohnbroo*
shout, to gritar *greetar*

show exposição *eh-eeshpoozeesaoon*
show, to mostrar *mooshtrar*
shower ducha (P) *dooshah*
chuveiro (B) *shooveh-eeroo*
sidewalk passeio da estrada
(P) *pahsehyoo dah shtrahdah* calçada
(B)*kahlsahdah*
signature assinatura
ahseenahtoorah
silver prata *prahtah*
simple *seemplesh*
since (e.g. since March)
desde *deshdeh*
sing, to cantar *kahntar*
singer cantor *kahntor*
single solteiro *sohlteh-eeroo*
sirloin lombo *lohnboo*
sister irmã *eermah*
sit down, to sentar *sehntar*
size número de roupa
noomehroo deh roh-oopah
skewers espetos *shpehtoosh*
skin pele *pehleh*
skirt saia *sayah*
sleep, to dormir *doormeer*
slice fatia *fahtee-ah*
sliced em fatias *ehn fahtee-ash*
slow lento *lehntoo*
small pequeno *pehkehnoo*
small dish pires *peeresh*
smell (sense of s.) olfato
ohlfahtoo

smoke fumo *foomoo*
smoke, to fumar *foomar*
smoked defumado
dehfoomahdoo
smoking fumador *foomahdor*
smooth liso *leezoo*
snails caracóis *kahrahkoh-eesh*
snow neve *nehveh*
snow, to nevar *nehvar*
so tanto *tahntoo*
soap sabão *sahbaoon*
soccer futebol *footehbohl*
soft mole *mohleh*
soja soja *sohjah*
sole solha *sohlyah*
some algum *ahlgoon*
someone alguém *ahlghen*
something alguma coisa
ahlgoon koh-eezah
son filho *feelyoo*
song canção *kahnsaoon*
soup sopa *sohpah*
sour azedo *ahzehdoo*
south sul *sool*
spaghetti esparguete
shpargehteh
speak, to falar *fahlar*
speed velocidade
vehlooseedahdeh
spend, to gastar *gashtar*
spinach espinafre
shpeenahfreh
sport desporto (P) *deshportoo*
esporte (B) *eeshportchee*

spring primavera
  preemahvehrah
squid lulas *loolash*
stadium estádio *shtahdee-oo*
stairs escadas *shkahdash*
stamp selo *sehloo*
stationery shop papelaria
  pahpehlahree-ah
stay, to sobrar *soobrar*
steak bife *beefeh*
steam vapor *vahpor*
stew estufado (P)
  shtoofahdoo picadinho (B)
  peekahdjeenyoo
still ainda *aheendah*
stockings meias *meh-eeash*
stomach estômago
  shtohmahgoo
stone pedra *pehdrah*
  precious s. preciosa
  prehsee-ohza
stop, to parar *parar*
stopped parado *parahdoo*
storm tempestade
  tehmpeshtahdeh; temporal
  tehmpoorahl
straw (for drinking) palhinha
  (P) *pahlyeenyah* canudinho
  (B) *kahnoodjeenyo*
strawberry morango *moo-rahngoo*
street estrada *shtrahdah;* rua
  roo-ah
strong forte *forteh*

strudel strudel *stroodehl*
student estudante
  shtoodahnteh
stuffing recheio *resheh-ee-oo*
subway métro (P) *mehtroo*
  metrô (B) *mehtroh*
sucking pig leitão *leh-eetaoon*
sugar açúcar *ahsookar*
suit fato (P) *fahtoo* terno (B)
  ternoh
suitcase mala *mahlah*
summer verão *veraoon*
sun glasses óculos de sol
  ohkooloosh deh sohl
sun sol *sol*
Sunday domingo
  doomeengoo
sunstroke insolação
  eensoolasaoon
supermarket supermercado
  soopermerkahdoo
supper jantar *jahntar*
sure certo *sertoo*
surgelato congelado
  kohnjehlahdoo
surname sobrenome
  sohbrehnohmeh **maiden n.**
  de solteira *deh solteh-eerah*
sweet doce *dohsseh*
sweet-and-sour agridoce
  ahgreedohseh
sweetener adoçante
  ahdoosahnteh

swim, to nadar *nahdar*
swimming pool piscina
 peesheenah
switch interruptor
 eenterooptor
syrup xarope *sharohpeh*

T-shirt t-shirt
table mesa *mehzah*
table napkin guardanapo
 gwardahnahpoo
tablecloth toalha *too-ahlyah*
tablespoon colher *koolyer*
tablet pastilha *pashteelyah*
take, to pegar *pehgar*
talcum powder pó de talco
 poh deh tahlkoo
tangerine tangerina
 tahnjereenah
tap torneira *toorneh-eerah*
tariff tarifa *tareefah*
taste, to provar *proovar*
tavern taverna, tasca
 tahvernah, tashkah
tax imposto *eemposhtoo*
taxi táxi *taksee*
tea (afternoon snack)
 merenda, lanche
 merehndah, lahnsheh
tea bag saquinho de chá
 sahkeenyoo deh shah
tea chá *shah*
teach, to ensinar *ehnseenar*
teacher professor *proofessor*

tear (-drop) lágrima
 lahgreemah
teaspoon colher de chá
 koolyer deh shah
telegram telegrama
 tehlehgrahmah
telephone telefone
 tehlehfohneh
telephone booth telefone
 público (P) *tehlehfohneh
 poobleekoo* orelhão (B)
 ohrehlyaoon
telephone call chamada (P)
 shahmahdah telefonema (B)
 tehlehfohnehmah
telephone directory lista
 telefônica *leeshtah
 tehlehfohneekah*
television televisão
 tehlehveezaoon
telex telex *tehleks*
temperature temperatura
 tehmpehrahtoorah
tender tenro *tehnroo*
tennis tênis *tehneesh*
tent cortinado (P)
 koorteenahdoo cortina (B)
 korteenah
terrace terraço *terrahsoo*
thank you obrigado
 ohbreegahdoo
thank, to agradecer
 ahgrahdehser
that aquele *ahkehleh;* que *keh*

theater teatro *teh-ahtroo*
then então *ehntaoon*
there ali *ahlee*
therefore depois (P) *dehpoh-eesh* e aí (B) *ee ah-ee*
thermometer termômetro *termohmehtroo*
they eles (*m*) *ehlesh*, elas (*f*) *ehlash*
thief ladrão *lahdraoon*
thin fino *feenoo;* magro *mahgroo*
think, to pensar *pehnzar*
third terceiro *terseh-eeroo*
thirst sede *sehdeh*
this este *eshteh*
this evening hoje à noite *ohjeh ah noh-eeteh*
thousand mil *meel*
thread linha *leenyah*
throat garganta *gargahntah*
through através *ahtrahvesh*
throw away, to jogar fora *joogar fohrah*
Thursday quinta-feira *keentah feh-eerah*
ticket bilhete *beelyehteh*
ticket office bilheteria *beelyehtehree-ah*
tide maré *mareh*
tie (neck t.) gravata *grahvahtah*
time tempo *tehmpoo;* vez *vesh* **once upon a**

time uma vez *era oomah vesh*
timetable horário *oraree-oh*
tin caixa *kah-eeshah;* lata *lahtah*
tip gorjeta *goorjehtah*
tire (*n.*) pneu *pneh-oo*
tired cansado *kahnsahdoo*
toast (when drinking) brinde *breendeh*
toasted torrado *toorahdoo*
tobacco tabaco *tahbahkoo*
tobacconist tabacaria *tahbahkaree-ah*
today hoje *ohjeh*
together juntos *joontoosh*
toilet paper papel higiênico *pahpehl eejee-ehneekoo*
tomato tomate *toomahteh*
tomorrow amanhã *ahmahnyah*
tongue língua *leengwah*
too (much) demais *dehmah-eesh*
tooth dente *dehnteh*
toothbrush escova de dentes *shkohva deh dehntesh*
toothpaste pasta de dentes *pashtah deh dehntesh*
toothpick palito *pahleetoo*
total total *tootahl*
tourism turismo *tooreeshmoh*
tourist turista *tooreeshtah*

towel toalha de mão *too-ahlyah deh maoon*
track pista *peeshtah*
traditional tradicional *trahdeesee-oonahl*
traffic trânsito *trahnseetoo*
train comboio (P) *kohmboh-ee-oo* trem (B) *trehn*
tram elétrico (P) *eelehtreekoo* bondinho (B) *bohndjeenyoo*
tranquillizer calmante *kahlmahnteh*
translate, to traduzir *trahdoozeer*
translation tradução *trahdoosaoon*
travel agent agente de viagem *adjehnteh deh veeahjehn*
travel, to viajar *vee-ahjar*
tray vaso *vahzoo*
tree árvore *ahrvoo-reh*
trip excursão *eh-eeshkoorsaoon*
tripe tripa *treepah*
trolley carrinho *kareenyoo*
trout truta *trootah*
true verdadeiro *verdahdeh-eeroo*
trunk cofre *kohfreh;* porta bagagens *portah bahgahjehnsh*
try, to provar *proovar*

tunafish atum *ahtoon*
tunnel túnel *toonehl*
turkey perú *pehroo*
turn off, to apagar *ahpahgar*
turnip nabo *nahboo*
type gênero *jehneroo*
typical típico *teepeekoh*

umbrella guarda-chuva *gwardah shoovah*
uncertain indeciso *eendeseezoo*
uncle tio *tee-oo*
uncomfortable incômodo *eenkohmoodoo*
undefined indefenido *eendehfehneedoo*
under em baixo *ehn bah-eeshoo*
underpants cuecas *kwehkash*
understand, to perceber (P) *persehber* entender (B) *ehntehnder*
underwear roupa interior (P) *roh-oopah eentehree-or* lingerie (B) *lahnjehree*
undo, to desfazer *deshfahzer*
unfortunately infelizmente *eenfehleeshmehnteh*
unique único *ooneekoo*
unite, to unir *ooneer*
unity unidade *ooneedahdeh*
university universidade *ooneeverseedahdeh*

urgent urgente *oordjehnteh*
us nós *nosh*
use uso *oozoo*
use, to usar *oozar*
used to, to be ser
  acustumado *sehr
  akooshtoomahdoo*
useful útil *ooteel*

valid válido *vahleedoo*
vanilla baunilha *bah-
  ooneelyah*
veal vitela *veetehlah*
vegetable (side dish)
  acompanhamento
  ahkohnpahnyamehntoo
vegetable garden horta *orta*
vegetables hortaliças (P)
  ortahleesash verduras (B)
  verdoorash; legumes
  lehgoomesh
vegetarian vegetariano
  vehjehtahree-ahnoo
video video *veedeh-oo*
village aldeia *ahldeh-ee-ah*
vinegar vinagre *veenahgreh*
visa visto *veeshtoo*
visit, to visitar *veezeetar*
vitamine vitamina
  veetahmeenah
voi vocês *vohsesh*

waistcoat colete *koolehteh*
wait, to esperar *eeshpehrar*

waiter empregado
  ehmprehgahdoo
waiting room sala de espera
  sahlah deh shperah
wake, to acordar *akoordar*
walk passeio *pahseh-ee-oo*
wall parede *parehdeh*
wallet carteira, porta-moedas
  *karteh-eerah, porta-moo-
  ehdash*
want, to querer *kehrehr*
wardrobe guarda-roupa (P)
  gwardah roh-oopah armário
  (B) *armaree-oo*
warn, to avisar *ahveezar*
wash basin lavatório
  lahvahtohree-oo
wash, to lavar *lahvar*
washing machine máquina
  de lavar roupa *mahkeenah
  deh lahvar roh-oopah*
water água *ahgwah* **mineral**
  mineral *meenehrahl* **fizzy**
  com gás *kohn gash* **natural**
  natural *nahtoorahl* **drinking**
  potável *pootahvehl* **tap** da
  torneira *dah toorneh-eerah*
  tonic tônica *tohneekah*
watercress agrião *ahgree-
  aoon*
watermelon melancia
  mehlahnsseeah
waterproof impermeável
  eenpermeh-ahvehl

wave onda *ohndah*
wax cera *cherah*
way modo *mohdoo*
weak fraco *frahkoo*
weakness fraqueza
  frahkehzah
wedding casamento
  kahzahmehntoo
Wednesday quarta-feira
  kwartah feh-eerah
week semana *sehmahnah*
weekend fim-de-semana *feen
  deh sehmahnah*
weight peso *pehzoo*
welcome bem-vindo *behn
  veendoo*
well bem *behn*
West oeste *oh-eshteh*
wet molhado *moolyahdoo*
when quando *kwandoo*
where aonde, onde *ah-
  ohndeh, ohndeh*
which qual *kwal*
while enquanto *ehnkwahntoo*
whisky uísque *weeskeh*
white branco *brahnkoo*
whiting badejo *bahdehjoo*
who quem *kehn*
whole inteiro *eenteh-eeroo*
wide largo *largoo*
width largura *largoorah*
wife esposa *shpohzah*
wild selvagem
  sehlvahjehn

wind vento *vehntoo*
window janela *jahnehlah*
windscreen pára-brisas
  parah-breezash
windsurf windsurf
wine vinho *veenyoo*
winter inverno *eenvernoo*
with com *kohn*
without sem *sen*
woman mulher *moolyer*
wood bosque *boshkeh*
wool lã *lahn*
word palavra *pahlahvrah*
work trabalho *trahbahlyoo*
**work, to (of a
  mechanism)** funcionar
  foonsyoonar; trabalhar
  trahbahlyar
worried preocupado *preh-
  ohkoopahdoo*
worse pior *pee-or*
wounded ferido *fereedoo*
wrap, to envolver
  ehnvohlvehr
write, to escrever *shkrehver*

yacht iate *yahteh*
year ano *ahnoo*
yeast fermento *fermehntoo*
yellow amarelo *ahmahrehloo*
yes sim *seen*
yesterday ontem *ohntehn*
yoga ioga *yohgah*
yoghurt iogurte *yogoort*

you tu *too*
young jovem *johvehn*
youth hostel albergue da
  juventude *ahlbergeh dah
  joovehntoodeh*
youth juventude
  joovehntoodeh

zero zero *zehroo*
zip code código postal (P)

  kohdeegoo poostahl cep (B)
  sehp
zipper fecho-éclair (P)
  feshoo ehseh-eer zíper (B)
  zeeper
zoo jardim zoológico
  *jardeen zoo-
  ohlohjeekoo*
zucchini abobrinha
  ahbohbreenyah

à americana see Gastronomic Terms, p. 24

à andaluza see Gastronomic Terms, p. 24

à belle munière see Gastronomic Terms, p. 24

à caçadora see Gastronomic Terms, p. 24

à Califórnia see Gastronomic Terms, p. 24

à moda de see Gastronomic Terms, p. 24

à provençal see Gastronomic Terms, p. 24

abacate avocado pear

abacaxi (B) pineapple

aberto open

abóbora pumpkin, see Regional Dishes, p. 36 **com camarão seco** see Regional Dishes, p. 47

abobrinha zucchini

abraçar to hug

abraço hug

abre garrafas bottle opener

abre latas can opener

abril April

absorvente *noun* sanitary towel

acabar to finish

açafrão saffron

acampar to camp

acarajé (B) see Regional Dishes, p. 47

acelerar to accelerate

acender to light

aceso lit, lighted

achar to find

acidente accident

ácido acid

aço steel

acontecer to happen

açorda (P) see National Dishes, p. 28 **de camarão (P)** see Recipes, p. 58 **de mariscos** see Regional Dishes, p. 38

Açores archipelago of the Azores

açougue (B) butcher

açúcar sugar

açucareiro sugar bowl

adiantado leftover

adoçante sweetener

adulto adult

advogado lawyer

aeroporto airport

afastar to go/send away

agência agency

agitar bem antes de usar shake well before use

agora now

agosto August

agradecer to thank

agradecimento thanks

agridoce sweet-and-sour see Gastronomic Terms, p. 24

água mineral mineral

water **natural** natural **com gás** fizzy **sem gás** without gas

aguardente brandy

agulha needle **e linha** and thread

aí dunque, then

ainda again/still

aipim frito (B) see Regional Dishes, p. 51

aipo celery

ajudar to help

alandroal (P) see Cheeses, p. 9

alarme alarm

albergue da juventude youth hostel

alcachofra artichoke

alcaparras capers

alcoólico alcoholic

aldeia village

além as well **além do mais** among other things

Alentejo area in southern Portugal

alergia allergy

aletria (P) see Sweets and Pastries, p. 14

alface lettuce

alfaiate tailor

Algarve area in the far south of Portugal

algodão cotton

alguém someone

algum any(one) no(-one)

alguma coisa something

alguns some

alheiras (P) see Preserved Meats, p. 12

alho garlic

ali there

alimentação food, diet

alimento food

almoço lunch

almofada cushion

almôndegas meatballs see Regional Dishes, p. 54 **de lebre** see Regional Dishes, p. 36

alô! (B) hello! (on the phone)

alto tall, high

alto! stop!

aluguel rent

amanteigado buttered

amarelo yellow

amargo bitter

amarguinha (P) see Wines and Spirits, p. 17

ambiente environment

amêijoas clams, see Regional Dishes, p. 38, 42

ameixa plum

amêndoa almond

amendoins peanuts

amido starch

amigo friend

amora blackberry

amortecedor bumpers
analcoólico non-alcoholic
ananás (P) pineapple
anchova anchovy
ancião elderly
andar to walk
anel ring
angu de arroz nordestino, goiano (B) see Regional Dishes, p. 46, 49
anis aniseed
ano year
antes before
antibiótico antibiotic
antigamente in the past
antigo ancient
antiguidades antiquities
anular to cancel
anúncios advertisements
ao champignon see Gastronomic Terms, pag. 24
ao creme see Gastronomic Terms, pag. 25
ao curry see Gastronomic Terms, pag. 25
ao lado by the side
ao menos at least
aonde where
ao redor around
ao thermidor see Gastronomic Terms, pag. 25
apagar to turn off
apartamento apartment
a pé on foot

apenas just, hardly
aperitivo aperitif
apertado narrow, tight
apetite appetite
apólice de seguro insurance policy
apresentar to present, to introduce
aquário aquarium
aquecedor radiator (for central heating)
aquecer to heat
aquecimento heating
aquele that
aqui here
ar air **condicionado** air conditioning
areia sand
arenque herring
armário cupboard, wardrobe
aroma aroma, smell
arroz rice **à grega (B)** see National Dishes, p. 52 **com feijão (B)** see National Dishes, p. 30 **com guariroba (B)** see Regional Dishes, p. 49 **de alhos, de grelos ou de brócolis** see National Dishes, p. 38 **de cabidela (P)** see Recipes, p. 59 **de carreteiro (B)** see Regional Dishes, p. 55 **de côco (B)** see Regional Dishes, p. 46 **de lapas (P)**

see Regional Dishes, p. 44
de pato (P) see Regional Dishes, p. 33 **de polvo (P)** see Regional Dishes, p. 42
do povo (B) see Regional Dishes, p. 49 **doce (P)** see Sweets and Pastries, p. 14
mineiro (B) see Regional Dishes, p. 51
árvore tree
asa wing
aspargos asparagus
aspirina aspirin
assado roast, see Gastronomic Terms, p. 25, **de peixe** see Regional Dishes, p. 40
assinatura signature
até until
atenção attention
atletismo athletics
atrás back
atrasado late
através through
atum tunafish **assado (P)** see Regional Dishes, p. 43
atum ou peixe-espada grelhado (P) see National Dishes, pag. 28
autêntico true
autocarro (P) bus
autorização authorisation
aveia oats
avelã hazelnut

avenida avenue
avião airplane
avisar to advise, to warn
azar bad luck
azeitão (P) see Cheeses, p. 9
azeite olive oil
azeitonas olives
azul blue
azulejo ornamental tile

baba-de-moça (B) see Sweets and Pastries, p. 14, Recipes, p. 60
bacalhau salted cod **à Assis, à Bras, à Gomes de Sá, à Margarida da Praça, à Zé do Pipo, assado com batatas a murro, de São Martinho**, see Regional Dishes (P), p. 33, 37, 39, 43 and Recipes, p. 61
bacon defumado smoked bacon
badejo whiting
bagaço (P) see Wines and Spirits, p. 17
bailarina ballerina
bairrada (P) see Wines and Spirits, p. 17
baixo low, short
bala (B) candy
bala bullet
balão ball
banana banana

bananas fritas (B) see Other
  Specialties, p. 22
banco bank
banco stool
band aid sticking plaster
banheiro (B) bathroom, toilet
banho bath
bar bar
barato economical
barba beard
barco boat
barman waiter
barulhento noisy
barulho noise
batata sotê (B) see Regional
  Dishes, p. 52
batatas potatoes **de Caçoilas
  (P)** see Regional Dishes,
  p. 37
batizado baptism
baton lipstick
baunilha vanilla
bebé baby
beber to drink
bebida drink
beco sem saída dead-end
  street
beijar to kiss
beijo kiss
beliche berth, bunk
bem well
benefícios benefits,
  advantages
benvindo welcome

berinjela eggplant
beterraba beetroot
bexiga see Preserved Meats,
  p. 12 and Regional Dishes,
  p. 35
bica (P) Expresso coffee
bife steak, veal slice, see
  Regional Dishes, p. 53 **à
  Cavalo (B) à marrare (P)**
  see Regional Dishes, p. 39
**bifes de atum com tomate
  (P)** pieces of tunafish, see
  Recipes, p. 62 **de atum em
  cebolada (P)** see Regional
  Dishes, p. 42
bilhete card, note **de
  identidade (P)** ID card
biscoito biscuit
bitoque (P) steak, fried eggs
  and chips
blaizer jacket
bobó de camarão (B) see
  Regional Dishes, p. 47
boca mouth
bocadinho (P) small piece
bocado a piece, a little
boi ox
bola ball **de berlim (P)**
  doughnut **de presunto** see
  Regional Dishes, p. 35 **de
  carne (P)** see Other
  Specialties, p. 22
bolinhos see Sweets and
  Pastries, p. 14 **de bacalhau**

169

(P) see National Dishes, p. 28 **de Jerimu** see Sweets and Pastries, p. 14

bolo dessert, cake **Rei (P)** typical Christmas pudding, see Sweets and Pastries, p. 14

bolsa bag

bombeiros fire-fighters

bondinho (B) tram

bonito beautiful

bordado embroidered cloth

botão button

botas boots

bovino bovine

braço arm

branco white

brigadeiro (B) see Sweets and Pastries, p. 14

brilhar to shine

brincos earrings

brinde toast (proposed when drinking)

brinquedos toys

broa (P) see Other Specialties, p. 22

brócolis broccoli

brodo de carne (P) see Regional Dishes, p. 43

brushing set (a hair-do)

bucelas (P) see Wines and Spirits, p. 18

burro donkey

buzina (motor-)horn

cabeça head

cabeleireiro hairdresser

cabide hangers

cabrito kid (young goat) **assado (P)** see Regional Dishes, p. 35 and Recipes, p. 63

cação dogfish

cacau cocoa

cachaça (B) aquavitae, see Wines and Spirits, p. 18

cachimbo pipe

cacholeira (P) see Preserved Meats, p. 12

cachorro (B) dog

cada each

cadeira chair

café coffee **com leite** coffee with milk

da manhã (B) breakfast

cair to fall

caixa cashier

caixa box

cajuzinhos (B) see Sweets and Pastries, p. 15

calças trousers

caldeirada fish soup **à Pescador (P)** see Regional Dishes, p. 39

caldo de cana (B) see Other Specialties, p. 22 **verde (P)** see National Dishes, p. 29

calmante tranquillizer

calmo calm

calor hot **que calor!** isn't it hot!
calorias calories
cama bed **de casal** double (bed) **de solteiro** single (bed)
camarão gambero **com côco (B)** see Regional Dishes, p. 46 and Recipes, p. 64 **frito (B)** see National Dishes, p. 30
camarões à paulista see Regional Dishes, p. 54
camisa shirt
camomila camomile
campo country(side)
canapés small savouries
canarinho canary, see Regional Dishes, p. 44
canção song
cancelar to cancel
canela cinnamon
caneta pen
canja chicken soup
canjica see Sweets and Pastries, p. 15
cansado tired
cantina canteen
cão dog
capacidade capacity
capaz able
caqui persimmon
cara face
caracóis snails, see Regional Dishes **(P)**, p. 39
caranguejo crab

carinho tenderness
carioca native of Rio de Janeiro
carne assada see National Dishes, p. 29 **de ganso à antiga (P)** see Regional Dishes, p. 44 **de porco com castanhas (P)** see Regional Dishes, p. 35 **de sol ou carne-seca(B)** see Other Specialties, p. 22 **de vinha d'alhos (P)** see Regional Dishes, p. 43 and Recipes, p. 65 **seca (B)** see carne de sol **seca com jerimum (B)** see Regional Dishes, p. 47
carneiro mutton **assado (P)** see Regional Dishes, p. 40
caro dear
carrinho do bebê pram **do supermercado** supermarket trolley
carro automobile
cartão de crédito credit card
carteira de identidade ID card
caruru (B) see Regional Dishes, p. 48
casaco loose jacket
casa de banho (P) bathroom, toilet
Casa de Calçada, Casal Garcia, Casal Mendes (P) see Wines and Spirits, p. 18

casca peel (of potato etc.)
casino casino
casquinhas de Siri (B) see
  National Dishes, p. 30
casquinhos de lagosta (B) see
  Regional Dishes, p. 46
castanhas chestnuts
castanho light brown
catupiry (B) see Cheeses, p. 10
caviar caviar
cebola onion
cego blind
ceia dinner (on feast-days)
celeiro canteen, cellar
cenoura carrot
central central **estação**
  central central station
centro center
cereal cereal
cérebro brain
cereja cherry
cerveja beer **clara**
  ale **escura/preta** dark beer
cevada barley
chá tea
chamada (P) telephone call
chapéu hat
charuto cigar
Château Duvalier (B) see
  Wines and Spirits, p. 18
chave key
chefe enough
chega! stop!
chegar arrive

cheio full
cheiro smell
cheque check
chiclete chewing gum
chicória chicory
chimarrão (B) see National
  Dishes, p. 55
chocolate chocolate
chope (B) draught beer
chouriço (P) blood sausage
  see Preserved Meats, p. 12
chouriços (P) see Preserved
  Meats, p. 13
churrasco (B) see Regional
  Dishes, p. 53 **à Gaúcha** see
  Regional Dishes, p. 56
chuva rain
chuveiro shower
cidade city
cientista scientist
cigarro cigarette
cinto belt
cintura waist
cinza ash
cinzeiro ashtray
cinzento gray
cirurgia surgery
clara de ovo eggwhite
claro clear
cliente client
cobertor blanket
cobrir to cover
cocada (B) see Sweets and
  Pastries, p. 15

côco coconut
codorniz quail
coelho rabbit **assado** see
  National Dishes, p. 56
cogumelo mushroom
cogumelos guisados (P) see
  Regional Dishes, p. 35
coisa thing
**colares (P) see Wines and
  Spirits**, p. 18
colchão mattress
colégio school
colete vest
colher spoon
comboio train
combustível gas
começo beginning
comer to eat
como how
cômodo comfortable
compota jam
comprar to buy
compras shopping
comprido long
comprimido medicine, pill
computador computer
comunicação
  communication
confiança trust
confirmar confirm
confortável comfortable
congelado frozen
conhaque cognac, see Wines
  and Spirits, pag. 19

conjunto group
conseguir to succeed
conservante preservative
constipação flu
consulado consulate
consumação food or drink (in
  a bar etc.)
conta bill
contente pleased
continuar to continue
contra against
controlar to check
convidado guest
convidar to invite
copo glass
cor color
cordeiro lamb
correio post
cortar to cut
costoleta cutlet
costureira dressmaker
couve cabbage **de Bruxelas**
  Brussels sprouts **flor**
  cauliflower **à mineira (B)**
  see National Dishes, p. 51
couvert starter, hors-d'oeuvre
coxa hip **de frango** chicken
  leg
cozido boiled **à portuguesa
  (P)** see National Dishes,
  p. 29 **de grão** see Regional
  Dishes, p. 42
cozinha kitchen
cozinhar to cook

cozinheiro chef
creme cream **de abacaxi (B)** pineapple cream, see Recipes, p. 66 **de camarão (B)** prawn cream, see Regional Dishes, p. 39
criança child
crocante crisp
croissant brioche
croquete croquette
crú raw
crustáceo seafood
cruzamento crossroad
cubos de gelo ice cubes
culpa fault, responsibility
cuscuz à Paulista (P) see Regional Dishes, p. 54
custar to cost
custo cost

damasco apricot
dançar to dance
dão (P) see Wines and Spirits, p. 19
dar to give
debaixo under(neath)
dedo finger
defumado smoked
deixar to leave
demais too (much, many)
dentadura denture
dentista dentist
dentro in
depois after

depositar to deposit
depósito deposit
descaca nozes nutcracker
descacar to peel
descafeinado (P) decaffeinated coffee
desengordurar to remove fat
desinfetar to disinfect
desmaiar to faint
devagar slowly
dever duty, task
dezembro December
dia day
diabético diabetic
diferente different
difícil difficult
diminuir to diminish **a velocidade** to slow down
direção direction
direita right (direction)
direito straight ahead
diretoria direction
discoteca discothèque
distância distance
dívida debt
dizer to tell, to say
doar to donate
doação donation
doce de ovos (P) see Sweets and Pastries, p. 15
documento document
doente ill (person)
dólar dollar
dom gift

dono proprietor
dor pain **de cabeça**
 headache **de estômago**
 stomach ache **de barriga**
 stomach ache
dourada sea brem
dourado golden
dourado grouper
Douro river which flows
 through the town of Porto
ducha shower
duro hard

elenco list
eletricidade electricity
elevador elevator
embaixada embassy
em baixo under(neath)
em cima over, above
em frente in front of
empadas de galinha see
 Regional Dishes, p. 40
empregado employee
emprego employment
empurrar to push
encher to fill
encontrar to find
encontro appointment
endereço (B) address
engano mistake
engarrafado bottled
enguia eel **à moda do**
 Ribatejo see Regional
 Dishes, p. 39

enquanto while
então then
entrada entry
entrar to enter
entre! Come in!
entrecosto entrecote steak
entrega a domicílio home
 delivery
envelope envelope
erro mistake
erva grass
ervilhas peas
escada rolante escalator
escadas stairs
escola school
escolher to choose
escova brush **de dentes**
 toothbrush
escova (B) hair-do
escrever to write
escuro dark
espadarte (P) sword fish
espargos asparagus **bravos**
 com ovos see Regional
 Dishes, p. 41
especialista expert
esperar to hope, to wait
esperto cunning
espetáculo show
espetada spit
espinafres spinach
esposa bride
esquecer to forget
esquentar to heat

esquerda left
estação station
estacionamento car park
estacionar to park
está lá! (P) Hello! (on the phone)
este this
esteticista beautician
estômago stomach
estopeta de atum (P) see Regional Dishes, p. 42
estou! (P) Hi!
estrada road, street
estrangeiro foreigner
estreito narrow
esvaziar to empty
etiqueta label
evitar to avoid
excursão excursion
experiência experience
externo outside

faca knife
faisão pheasant
família family
famoso famous
farinha flour
farinheiras (P) see Preserved Meats, p. 13
farmácia pharmacy
farofa (B) see Regional Dishes, p. 53
faróis headlights
fatura invoice

favas broad bean
favor favor
fazer to do, to make **o pedido** to order (in a restaurant)
fé faith (religion)
febras de porco slices of pork
fechado closed
fechar to close
feijão beans **branco com cabeça de porco, com peixe, manteiga, verde à Alentejana** see Regional Dishes, p. 41, 50, 51
feijoada a dish of beans see National Dishes, p. 30 **à carioca (B)** see Recipes, p. 67 **à Transmontana (P)** see Regional Dishes, p. 35
feio ugly
felicidade happiness
feliz happy
feriado public holiday
férias holidays
fermento yeast
ferver to boil
fervido boiled
festa party
fevereiro February
ficar to stay
fígado liver **de porco, de cebolada (P)** see Regional Dishes, p. 39
figos figs

filé (B) steak, see National Dishes, p. 30 **de peixe com molho de camarão** see National Dishes, p. 31
filha daughter
filho son
fim end **de ano (P)** New Year, New Year's Eve
final final
finalidade purpose
fino thin
fino (P) draught beer
flambado see Gastronomic Terms, p. 25
flocos flakes
flor flower
florista florist
fogo fire
fome hunger
forno oven
forte strong
fósforo match
fotografia photograph
fotógrafo photographer
framboesa raspberry
frango (B) chicken **à caipira, com catupiry, com creme de milho** see Regional Dishes, p. 51, 56
frequentemente often
fresco fresh
frigideira frying pan
frigorífico (P) refrigerator
frio cold

fritada (B) omelette **de carne** see Regional Dishes, p. 50
frito fried
fruta fruit **fresca** fresh **seca** dried
frutos do mar seafood
fumar to smoke
fundo bottom
futebol football

gabardine raincoat
galão (P) coffee with milk
galeto young cockerel see Regional Dishes, p. 56
galinha fowl
garagem garage
garçon waiter
garfo fork
garganta throat
garota (B) girl
garoto (B) boy
garrafa carafe
gasolina gasoline
gaspacho à alentejana (P) cold soup, see Recipes, p. 68
gatão (P) see Wines and Spirits, p. 19
gato cat
geladeira (B) refrigerator
gelado ice cream
gelatina gelatine
geléia jam see Sweets and Pastries, p. 15
gelo ice

gema de ovo egg yolk
gênero kind, type
gengibre juniper
genro son-in-law
gente people
ginginha (P) see Wines and
Spirits, p. 19
gola collar
gordo fat
gordura fat, greasy (of food)
gorduroso greasy
gorjeta tip
gostar to like, to love
grande large
grão corn **de-bico guisado
com ovos** see Regional
Dishes, p. 37
grátis free of charge
grávida pregnant
grelhado roast see
Gastronomic Terms, p. 26
gripe influenza
gritar to shout
groselha redcurrant
guarda chuva umbrella
guardanapo napkin **de papel**
paper n.
guarda roupa wardrobe
guisadu see Gastronomic
Terms, p. 26

habitante resident
hálito breath
harmonia harmony

haver to have
herança heredity
hino hymn
honesto honest
honra honor
hora hour
horário timetable
horóscopo horoscope
hortaliça vegetable
hóspede guest
humor mood

idade age
igreja church
igual same
igualmente equally
imediatamente immediately
impossível impossible
impressora printer
incluído included
incomodar to disturb, to
irritate
incômodo uncomfortable
indicação indication
indigestão indigestion
informar to inform
início beginning
**inhoque (B) com carne
assada** see Regional Dishes,
p. 54
inseto insect
integral integral,
wholemeal
inteligente intelligent

interessante interesting
interno internal, inside
intoxicação intoxication
inverno winter
invés de instead of
iogurt yoghurt
ir to go
já already
jacaré see Regional Dishes, p. 45
janeiro January
janela window
jantar supper
jardim garden
javali boar
jogar to play **fora** to throw away
jogo game
jornal newspaper
jovem young
julho July
juliana see Gastronomic Terms, p. 26
junho June
junto together

lã wool
laburdo (P) see Regional Dishes, p. 37
lago lagoon
lagos (P) see Wines and Spirits, p. 19
lagosta lobster **suada à moda de Peniche (P)** see Regional Dishes, p. 39
lagostins prawns
lampreia (P) lamprey, see Regional Dishes, p. 34
lanche snack
lápis pencil
laranja orange
laranjada orangeade
largar to leave
lavandaria laundry
lavar to wash
lebre hare
legal legal
lei law
leitão (B) piglet **assado** see Regional Dishes, p. 51
leite milk **condensado** condensed **desnatado** skimmed **creme (P)** see Recipes, p. 69
lenço handkerchief **de papel** paper handkerchief
lençol sheet
lentes a contato contact lenses
lentilhas (B) lentils **à moda de Minas** see Regional Dishes, p. 51
levar to take
leve light
licor liqueur
ligação call
limão lemon
limonada lemonade

limpo clean
lindo beautiful, handsome
língua language, tongue
linguiça sausage
linguiças see Preserved
Meats, p. 13
linha line
liso smooth
lista list **telefônica** telephone
directory
litro liter
livre free
livro book
local place
loja shop
lombinho (B) see Regional
Dishes, p. 56 **de porco
recheado** see Recipes, p. 70
lombo T-bone
louro bay leaf
louro/loiro blond
lua de mel honeymoon
lugar place
lulas calamary **cheias (P),
con ferrado (P)** see
Regional Dishes, p. 42
luvas gloves

maçã apple
maço de cigarros packet of
cigarettes
Madeira isle of Madeira
madeira (P) see Wines and
Spirits, p. 19

madeira wood
maduro ripe
mãe mother
magro thin
maionese mayonnaise
mais more
mal bad(ly) **entendido**
misunderstanding
mala suitcase
mamão papaya
mandioca manioca
maneira way
manga mango
manhã morning
manjar (B) see Sweets and
Pastries, p. 15
manjericão basil
manteiga butter, see
Gastronomic Terms, p. 26
mão hand
mar sea
março March
marido husband
marisco seafood
marmelada jam
marrom brown
mas but
massa pasta, pastry, dough
massa folhada puff pastry
mastigar to chew
Matheus Rosé (P) see Wines
and Spirits, p. 20
mau bad
Medalhão com arroz à

piemontese see National Dishes, p. 31
medicina medicine
médico doctor
medida size, measurement
meias stockings
mel honey
melancia watermelon
melão melon **com presunto with smoked ham**
melhor better
menos less
mensal monthly
mentira lie
menu menu
mercado market
mês month
mesa table
metade half
meter to put
mexilhão mussel
migas à Alentejana, ripadas (P) see Regional Dishes, p. 35, 41
mil thousand
milanesa see Gastronomic Terms, p. 26
milho maize **frito** see Regional Dishes, p. 43
Minho area in northern Portugal
minuto minute
miolo brain, see Regional Dishes, p. 41 **do pão** (fresh) breadcrumb

misto mixed
mistura mixture
miúdos offal
moeda coin
moedas (small) change
moer to mince, to chop
moído minced
molho sauce **de camarão** see Regional Dishes, p. 48
moluscos seafood
monumentos monuments
moqueca de peixe (B) see Regional Dishes, p. 48 and Recipes, p. 71
morada (P) address
morango strawberry
morcela blood sausage
moscatel (P) see Wines and Spirits, p. 20
mosquitos mosquitoes
mostarda mustard
mostrar to show
móveis furniture
muito much
mulher woman
muma de siri (B) see Regional Dishes, p. 50
museu museum
música music

nabo turnip
nacionalidade nationality
nada nothing
nadar to swim

não no
nariz nose
nascer to be born
natal Christmas
natas fresh cream
natureza nature
necessidade necessity
negociar to bargain
negro black
nem né, not even
nenhum nobody
nervoso nervous, tense
nevar to snow
ninguém nobody
**noisette see Gastronomic
  Terms**, pag. 26
noite night
noiva bride
nome name
norte north
nota fiscal invoice, receipt
notícia news
novembro November
novidade novelty
novo new
noz nut **moscada** nutmeg
nu nude
nublado cloudy
número number
nunca never **nunca mais!**
  never again
nutriente nutritious, filling
nutritivo nourishing
nuvem cloud

objetivo objective
obrigado thanks
obrigatório compulsory
obter to obtain
óculos glasses **de sol**
  sunglasses
ocupado occupied, busy
odor odor
oeste west
óleo seed oil **bronzeador**
  suntan oil
olho eye
ombro shoulder
omelete omelette see
  National Dishes, p. 29
o mesmo the same
onde where
ônibus (B) bus
ontem yesterday
orégano oregano
ostra oyster
ouro gold
outono autumn
outubro October
ouvir to listen, to hear
ovo egg **cozido** hard-boiled
  estrelado (P) fried **frito (B)**
  fried
ovos mexidos scrambled eggs

paca (B) see Regional
  Dishes, p. 49
pacote de cigarros pack of
  200 cigarettes

padaria breadshop
pagamento payment
pagar to pay
pai father
paios see Preserved Meats, p. 13
pais parents
país country
palavra word
palco stage
palito toothpicks
palmito (B) see Other Specialties, p. 22
panela saucepan
pão bread
pão-de-ló (P) see Sweets and Pastries, p. 15, **ralado** breadcrumbs
pãozinho de queijo (B) see Other Specialties, p. 23
papagaio parrot
papas de sarrabulho (P) see Regional Dishes , p. 34
. **papel higiênico** toilet paper
par pair
para for
parar to stop
parede wall
parente relative
pargo dentex
parmegiana see Gastronomic Terms, p. 26
parmesão parmesan
parque park

parte part
partido party (political)
partido broken
partir to leave **a partir de agora** from now on
páscoa Easter
passaporte passport
pasta de dentes toothpaste
pastel batter **de molho (P)** see Regional Dishes, p. 37 **de natas (P)** see Sweets and Pastries, p. 15 **de Santa Clara (P)** see Sweets and Pastries, p. 16
pastelão de Vila Velha see Regional Dishes, p. 56
pastelaria cakeshop
pataniscas de bacalhau see Regional Dishes, p. 40
pato duck
paulista native of São Paulo
pavê (B) see Sweets and Pastries, p. 16 **de pêssego** see Recipes, p. 72
pé foot
pedacinho (B) small piece
pedaço piece
pedido request
pedra de isqueiro flint for a lighter
pegar to take
peito de frango chicken breast
peixe fish **à Mato Grosso** see

Regional Dishes, p. 49 **à moda capixaba** see Regional Dishes, p. 50
espada sword fish **frito** see Regional Dishes, p. 46 **frito de Escabeche (P)** see Regional Dishes, p. 40
pena pain, suffering
penso higiênico (P) sanitary towel
pepino cucumber
pequeno small **almoço (P)** breakfast
pêra pear
perder to lose
perdiz partridge, see Regional Dishes, p. 49 **com cogumelos (P)** see Regional Dishes, p. 35 **frita à Outeiro** see Regional Dishes, p. 37
perfume fragrance, smell
pergunta question
perguntar to ask
periferia outskirts
perigo danger
perna leg
perto near
peru turkey **assado** see Regional Dishes, p. 36
pesado heavy
pescada cod
pescar to fish
pêssego peach

pessoa person
piano piano
picadinho de carne see Regional Dishes, p. 53
picante hot (spicy)
pickles pickles
piemontesa see Gastronomic Terms, p. 27
pílula pill
pimenta pepper
pimentão bell pepper
pior worse
pipoca popcorn
pirão (B) see Regional Dishes, p. 48
piscina swimming pool
pistache pistachio nut
pitu con côco (B) see Regional Dishes, p. 50
planta plant
pneu tire
poder to be able
polvo pulp **guisado (P)** see Regional Dishes, p. 44
pombo pigeon, see Regional Dishes, p. 45
pôr to put **a mesa** to lay the table **na conta de** to debit **no lixo** to throw away
porção portion
porco pig, pork
porém but
por favor please
porque why

porta door
porta-moedas purse
Porto (P) see Wines and
  Spirits, p. 20
possível possible
postal postcard
pouco little
praça plaza
praia beach
prato plate
prazer pleasure
precisar to need
preço price
preferir prefer
prego nail
prejuízo prejudice
preparar prepare
presunto ham
presunto see Preserved
  Meats, p. 13
preto black
primavera spring
primeiro first
primo cousin
procurar to look for, to try
pronto ready
próprio own
provar to taste
provençal see Gastronomic
  Terms, p. 27
puchero do Paraná (B) see
  Regional Dishes, p. 56
pudim pudding
puxar to pull

qual which
qualidade quality
qualquer any
quando when
quanto how much
quarta feira Wednesday
quarto quarter; bedroom
quase nearly
que that
quebrado (B) broken
quebrar to break
queijadas de Sintra (P) see
  Recipes, p. 73
queijo cheese **da Ilha (P) da
  Serra (P) Minas (B) Prato
  (B)** see Cheeses, p. 10;
  ralado grated cheese
queimado burnt
queimar to burn
quem who
quente hot **água quente** hot
  water
querido dear
**quiabo com carne moída
  (B)** see Regional Dishes,
  p. 52
quibe (B) see Regional
  Dishes, p. 55
quibebe (B) see Regional
  Dishes, p. 52
quindim (B) see Sweets and
  Pastries, p. 16
quinta (P) house in the
  country with some land

quinta feira Thursday

rabanadas (P) see Sweets and
  Pastries, p. 16
rabanetes radishes
rádio radio
ralado grated
rancho (P) see National
  Dishes, p. 29
rapariga (P) girl
rapaz (P) boy
rápido fast
rebuçado (P) candy
receita recipe
recheado filling, stuffing
reclamação complaint
reduzir to reduce
reembolso refund
refeição meal
região region
relação relation
religião religion
relógio watch, clock
remédio medicine
requeijão (B) see Cheeses,
  p. 10
reservado booked
reservar to reserve
resfriado *noun* cold
responder to answer
resposta *noun* answer
restaurar to restore
retornar to return
revéillon (B) New Year

revista magazine
ricota ricotta cheese see
  Cheeses, p. 11
rir to laugh
risada *noun* laugh
risoto risotto, see National
  Dishes, p. 31
robe dressing gown
rocambole (B) see Sweets
  and Pastries, p. 16
rodízio de massas (B) see
  Regional Dishes, p. 53
rojões kidney see Regional
  Dishes, p. 34 **à moda do
  Minho (P)** see Recipes, p. 74
rombo rhombus
rosé rosé see Gastronomic
  Terms, p. 27
roupa dress
roupão bathrobe
roupa velha (P) see Regional
  Dishes, p. 34
rua street

sábado Saturday
saber to know
sabor flavor
saboroso tasty
saco plástico plastic bag,
  shopper
saia skirt
saída exit
sair to go out
sal salt

salada salad **de coelhu bravo**
see Regional Dishes, p. 37
de frutas fruit salad **de
macarrão de palmito** see
National Dishes, p. 31
saleiro salt shaker
salgado salted
salmão salmon
salmonete mullet
salpicão (B) see Regional
Dishes, p. 53
salsa parsley
salsicha würstel
sálvia sage
sandálias sandals
sandes sandwich
sanduíche bread roll with
filling
santola large crayfish
sapataria shoeshop
sapateiro shoemaker
sapatos shoes
sarapatel (P) see Regional
Dishes, p. 41
sardinha sardine **(P)** see
National Dishes, p. 30
saudades nostalgia, missing
someone or something
saúde health
sauna sauna
seco dry
seda silk
sede thirst
segunda feira Monday

segundo second
selo stamp
semana week
semanal weekly
sempre always
senhor gentleman, **Sr.** Mr.
senhora lady, **Sra.** Mrs.
sentir to feel **falta** to miss
someone or something
serpa (P) see Cheeses, p. 11
serviço service
setembro September
sexta-feira Friday
sidra (B) see Wines and
Spirits, p. 21
significado meaning
silêncio silence
sim yes
simples simple
sítio (P) place **(B)** house in
the country with some land
só only
sobremesa dessert
socorro! help!
sofá sofa **cama** sofa-bed
soja soya
solha sole
sombra shadow
somente only
sonho (B) doughnut
sopa soup **à Alentejana (P)**
see Regional Dishes, p. 41
de alheiras (P) see National
Dishes, p. 36 **de beterraba**

(B) beetroot s., see Recipes, p. 75, **de cabeca de peixe** see Regional Dishes, p. 42 **de entulho (P)** see Regional Dishes, p. 40 **de civilhas** see Regional Dishes, p. 51 **de ervilhas** see Regional Dishes, p. 54 **de favas** see Regional Dishes, p. 38 **de macaxeira (B)** see Regional Dishes, p. 46 **de milho verde** see Regional Dishes, p. 57

sorte luck

sorvete sherbet

soutien bra

steak au poivre see Gastronomic Terms, p. 27

strogonoff (B) see Regional Dishes, p. 57

subir to go up

suco juice **de cana (B)** sugar cane juice

suíno pork

sujo dirty

sul south

sumo (P) juice

supermercado supermarket

tainha mullet

talheres cutlery

talho (P) butcher

talvez maybe

tâmaras dates (fruit)

também also

tampa lid

tangerina tangerine

tapete carpet

tapioca (B) see Sweets and Pastries, p. 16

tarde afternoon

tártaro see Gastronomic Terms, p. 27

tartaruga see Regional Dishes, p. 45

tecido fabric

telefone telephone

telefonista telephone operator

temperatura temperature

tempo weather

ter to have

terça feira Tuesday

terceiro third

tesoura scissors

testa forehead

tipo kind

tirar to take off

toalha cloth **de banho** beach towel **de mão** towel **de mesa** tablecloth

todo all, whole, complete

toilette toilet, restroom

tomate tomato

toranja grapefruit

torrada crouton

torresmos fried scraps of pork fat **da Beira** see

INDEX

In the same series: